THE
DREAM
MANAGER

D0099301

Other Works by Matthew Kelly

The Rhythm of Life

The Seven Levels of Intimacy

Perfectly Yourself

The

DREAM
MANAGER

◆

MATTHEW KELLY

HYPERION NEW YORK

The Dream Manager, The Dream Manager Program,
and the Dream Book are registered trademarks of Floyd Consulting.

Copyright © 2007 Beacon Publishing

All rights reserved.
No part of this book may be used or reproduced in any
manner whatsoever without the written permission of the Publisher.
Printed in the United States of America. For information address
Hyperion, 77 West 66th Street, New York, New York 10023-6298.

Library of Congress Cataloging-in-Publication Data

Kelly, Matthew
   The dream manager / Matthew Kelly.—1st ed.
      p.   cm.

   ISBN-13: 978-1-4013-0370-9
   ISBN-10: 1-4013-0370-6
   1. Personnel management. 2. Organizational effectiveness.
3. Employee motivation. I. Title.
   HF5549.K3494 2007
   658.3'14—dc22   2007013597

Hyperion books are available for special promotions, premiums, or corporate
training. For details contact Michael Rentas, Proprietary Markets,
Hyperion, 77 West 66th Street, 12th floor,
New York, New York 10023, or call 212-456-0133.

Design by Victoria Hartman

FIRST EDITION

1   3   5   7   9   10   8   6   4   2

To my brother Simon—
my first Dream Manager!
Thanks for encouraging me
to dream the big dreams
when I was so young . . .

Go confidently in the direction of your dreams.
Live the life you have imagined!

—THOREAU

Foreword

THE MOST POWERFUL ideas are almost always the simple ones. And so often, they come from unlikely sources. Matthew Kelly's *The Dream Manager* is a testament to both of these axioms.

As long as organizations have existed, leaders have been looking for ways to inspire workers and keep them from leaving for imagined greener pastures. But during the past thirty years, as fewer and fewer people cling to the notion of staying with the same company for their entire careers, concerns about inspiring and retaining employees have grown rapidly. Today, with the increasing shortage of skilled labor in the job market—and the unprecedented leverage that it has given employees—the search for an effective solution to the retention problem in the corporate world has become nothing short of an obsession. And for good reason.

Executives today realize that the cost of losing good people is no longer limited to higher recruiting and retraining expenses; it is a recipe for failure. Even the most cynical manager will admit that one of the most important competitive advantages a company can have is the ability to keep and motivate the human capital that is in such short supply.

Unfortunately, managers and human resources professionals have traditionally focused most of their attention on levers like compensation and benefits. They've raised salaries, increased bonuses, awarded stock options, increased vacation time, and let people bring their pets to work—with limited success, at best. In those cases where a company has been able to successfully use one of these tools to coax an unfulfilled employee into staying, they usually find that the solution is only a temporary—and costly—one.

The truth is, few people—if any—work for money alone. Sure, we all need money, and we certainly factor it into our decisions about a given job. But when it comes to inspiring people and creating the kind of environment where employees laugh at the notion of leaving their company, there is something far more powerful—and less expensive—that companies have largely overlooked.

Until now.

As you read this book, you'll probably have the same reaction I did. "Why hasn't someone already figured this out? It's so obvious in hindsight!" And that is the sign of a truly ingenious idea.

And the real beauty of Matthew Kelly's breakthrough idea is that it is one of those rare discoveries that is as beneficial for employees as it is for a company's bottom line. It's like discovering a cheap and powerful new source of fuel that is also good for the environment!

The one sad thing about Matthew's idea—although I suppose from a competitive standpoint it might be a good thing—is that some managers will probably dismiss his theory. They might say, "Give me a break. That's the simplest idea I've ever heard." Or they'll think, "Who is this Matthew Kelly guy, anyway? He's not a business or management expert I've ever heard of."

My response to both of those objections is, "Exactly!"

—PATRICK LENCIONI
author of *The Five Dysfunctions of a Team*

employees as it is for a company's bottom line. It's like discovering a cheap and powerful new source of fuel that is also good for the environment!

The one sad thing about Matthew's idea—although I suppose from a competitive standpoint it might be a good thing—is that some managers will probably dismiss his theory. They might say, "Give me a break. That's the simplest idea I've ever heard." Or they'll think, "Who is this Matthew Kelly guy, anyway? He's not a business or management expert I've ever heard of."

My response to both of those objections is, "Exactly!"

—PATRICK LENCIONI
author of *The Five Dysfunctions of a Team*

THE
DREAM
MANAGER

THE DILEMMA

———————— ✦ ————————

THE FUTURE OF your organization and the potential of your employees are intertwined; their destinies are linked.

An organization can only become the-best-version-of-itself to the extent that the people who drive that organization are striving to become better-versions-of-themselves. This is universally true whether the organization is a business, a school, a government, a nonprofit, or a sports team. To the extent that a CEO, an executive team, and a group of managers and employees explore their potential as individuals, so too will an organization explore its potential.

The problem is, the great majority of people in the workplace today are *actively disengaged*. This is the dilemma that modern managers face. To varying extents, people don't feel connected to their work, the organizations they work in, or the people they work with. No single factor is affecting morale, efficiency, productivity, sustainable growth, customer intimacy, and profitability more than this *disengagement*.

Disengagement. Is an employee 85 percent engaged? 60 percent engaged? 50 percent engaged? Or worst of all, have they decided to "quit and stay"? You do the math. What does your payroll amount to? If on average your employees are 75 percent engaged, disengagement is costing you 25 percent of your payroll every month in productivity alone. The real cost to your business is of course much higher when you take into account how disengaged employees negatively affect your customers and every aspect of your business.

It has been almost forty years since Peter Drucker observed the single greatest error and deception of our accounting system: people are placed in the liability column on the balance sheet. Machinery and computers are categorized as assets and people as liabilities. The reality, of course, is that *the right people* are an organization's greatest asset. We may have acknowledged this truth in theory, but we have not allowed it to sufficiently penetrate the way we manage our organizations, and indeed, the way we manage the people who drive them.

It's not that we don't want to engage the people who work with us and for us. In most cases it seems that we simply have not found a practical, efficient, and affordable way to do it.

The Dream Manager concept provides a revolutionary way of reversing this crippling trend toward disengagement and demonstrates how organizations large and small can *actively engage* their people once again, thus creating a competitive advantage of monumental proportions.

In the past, companies have battled over price, quality, quantity, customer service, operational excellence, and product leadership. In the coming decades, we will witness the next great corporate battle—the war for talent. The battle may seem to be raging already to some, but in truth it is only just beginning.

BusinessWeek reports that, over the next ten years, 21 percent of top management and 24 percent of all management jobs across all functions, regions, and industries will become vacant. Add to this trend an aging population, a shrinking workforce, and a growing intolerance for the illegal immigrant population that provides much of the unskilled labor in the United States today, and you have a talent and labor crisis of enormous consequence across all disciplines—from the highly skilled to the completely unskilled.

But it is not enough simply to hire the right people. The ability to attract, engage, and retain talent will be the number one strategic objective of every successful modern leader and organization.

A football coach's number one priority is to attract, develop, nurture, organize, and motivate the franchise's talent. Coaches and team owners are intimately aware that the future success of their organization depends on the talent they attract, engage, and retain. Finding and nurturing talent is their number one priority. Why should the priorities of a CEO or manager be any different?

A company's purpose is to become the-best-version-of-itself.

The next question is: What is an employee's purpose? Most would say, "to help the company achieve its purpose," but they would be wrong. That is certainly part of an employee's role, but an employee's primary purpose is to become the-best-version-of-himself or herself. Contrary to unwritten management theory and popular practice, people do not exist for the company. The company exists for people. When a company forgets that it exists to serve its customers, it quickly goes out of business. Our employees are our first customers, and our most influential customers.

A person's purpose is to become the-best-version-of-himself or herself.

Finding a way to create an environment that helps employees become the-best-version-of-themselves, while at the same time moving the company toward the-best-version-of-itself, may seem impossible to many; to others, these purposes may seem diametrically opposed; but in reality, they are astoundingly complementary.

This is the story of how one leader and his executive team set out to transform a business by *actively engaging a disengaged workforce.*

The secret revealed within this story unveils the very core of what drives us as human beings, not only at work, but in every arena of our lives. So whether you are the CEO of a large corporation or the leader of a small department, the principal of a school or a football coach, a parent grappling with the dynamics of teamwork within your family or an employee just looking to make sense of the work you do every day . . . you are about to discover something that will change your life forever.

PART ONE

———— ◆ ————

DESPERATION

Just Another Day

Something was wrong and Simon Roberts knew it. Meandering slowly through traffic on another cloudy morning, he started wondering where his life was going, and his thoughts quickly wandered to his job. It seemed so transactional now, and that left him feeling flat and unmotivated. Simon wasn't a lazy person; he loved a good challenge. But lately he'd found himself disengaging from his work, and that bothered him. Something needed to change—he just wasn't sure what it was, or where to start.

He had joined Admiral Janitorial Services four years earlier because solving problems and working with people were the two things Simon was passionate about.

His business card read "General Manager," but as Simon

reflected on the past four years, it seemed he had spent most of his time dealing with recruiting issues. "Lead Recruiter" seemed more accurate since, truth be told, 75 percent of his time was spent dealing with issues directly related to the "T" word.

"Turnover," that is. But at Admiral, you didn't speak that word.

Sure, plenty of companies have turnover problems nowadays, and building a team has perhaps never been more difficult. But if you think *your* company has a turnover problem, try getting people to clean toilets. That's what Simon had spent most of his time working on over the past four years. Admiral Janitorial Services had just over four hundred employees and an annual turnover rate of 400 percent, just above the industry average. Needless to say, team spirit and employee morale were low.

Pulling into his parking space at Admiral's headquarters, Simon felt his energy plummet and wondered how he would face another day. All he could hear was a *Winnie-the-Pooh* tape his son used to listen to as a child playing over and over in his mind, and it was stuck on the line, "If you do what you've always done, you'll get what you've always gotten."

How Much Is Turnover Costing Us?

"It's costing me a fortune," Greg said as he charged through the door. He never had learned to knock, but then again, he owns the company.

Greg founded Admiral when he was just seventeen and,

over the past twenty-five years, he has grown the business from a one-man operation to a small army of around four hundred employees.

Today, he is a successful and wealthy businessman, but whenever people ask him what he does, he always replies, "I'm a janitor." From time to time, he will attend a black-tie affair and people will laugh at his answer, thinking he is joking. But discovering he is serious, their laughter quickly diminishes into embarrassment.

Greg is an entrepreneur—he can sell anything to anyone and has an uncanny ability to see trends and opportunities long before anybody else. But he can also be a little scattered and a bit of a hothead, and that's why Simon was hired as general manager four years ago.

"What's costing you a fortune?" Simon volleyed, though he knew exactly what Greg was talking about.

"Turnover!" Greg said, visibly exasperated.

On Friday afternoon, Simon had left the month-end reports on Greg's desk. Among those reports were the quarterly turnover numbers. Over the last three months, Admiral's turnover had been 107 percent. That's right. In the past ninety days, 428 employees had left Admiral.

"It's hard to know how much this is costing us," Simon said. "We are having to hire for some positions three times a quarter. And it's not just recruitment costs. Turnover affects morale, efficiency, and customer relationships. I've been telling you for twelve months that it's a big problem."

Greg nodded. "I know, I know. It's just that now we're starting to lose clients over it. I had a call from Charlie down at P & G today, telling me we're getting a warning letter putting us on a ninety-day probationary period. He says our work has been sloppy and they've noticed a constant flow of new faces, and they feel like things are falling between the cracks."

Simon just sat there, staring at Greg in a bit of a daze.

Greg continued, "So you've got my attention. Give them a pay raise, won't that make them stay?"

"I wish it would, but I'm not sure," Simon replied. "I don't want to just throw money at the problem. Let's find out what's causing the turnover. Let's find out why they're leaving."

"How will we find that out?" Greg asked.

"We'll ask them," said Simon.

"Huh!" grunted Greg. Clearly, this idea had never occurred to him.

Ask Your Employees

The next morning, Simon and Greg met at First Watch to talk more about their turnover problem. It was a relaxed environment, the food and service were great, and that made it Simon's favorite place for breakfast meetings.

"So you're just going to go around and ask them why people are leaving?" inquired Greg, half serious and half sarcastic.

"Let's remember, Greg, they know things about our business that we don't know. I read an article last month about the president of American Airlines. Refueling costs were killing them, especially at airports where they had to contract other airlines to refuel their planes. One day he was pondering the problem after a meeting with his executive team that went nowhere. So he drove out to Fort Worth from his office in downtown Dallas, went down to maintenance, got a couple of crews together, told them the problem, and asked them what they thought the solution was.

"They just looked at each other. Some smiled, some just shook their heads. They all knew the answer. Put enough fuel in the planes while they are in Dallas to fly to and from Los Angeles. The plane will use a little more fuel, and if delayed you may need a top-up in LA, but it will still be cheaper than contracting a third party to refuel the planes in LA. In the next twelve months, American Airlines saved millions of dollars because of this single idea . . . even with the rising cost of fuel."

Greg sat there pondering as Simon continued. "The employees know things about our business that we don't. We should do a survey and ask them why they think so many people come and go."

"A survey? How much will that cost?" Greg asked, always obsessed with the bottom line.

Shrugging his shoulders, Simon said, "I don't know yet, but I know it will be worth it. You'll be amazed at what they'll tell us. Nobody knows the business like those who work in the trenches of it every single day. Ask your employees. They know more than you think."

The Initial Survey

Simon spent the next week working up a few simple questions for the survey. He had just one goal in mind: to discover why so many employees came and went at Admiral.

The following Monday morning, the surveys were distributed to each of Admiral's 407 employees.

At first, the employees were resistant. Some were cynical, others were skeptical, and most of them were just plain cautious. Who could blame them? It was out of left field. It was just so different from what they were used to.

"Why are they asking me why people are leaving? Why don't they ask the people who left?" Simon overheard one employee saying in the lunchroom.

A few brave shift managers came by Simon's office to ask him straight out what he was trying to get at. Simon set them at ease, asked them to be sincere, and asked them to encourage their direct reports to do the same.

"They don't have to put their names on the surveys. They can just fill them out and hand them back," he explained. "Like I said in my letter on the front page of the survey, we can't go on like this, month after month, hiring dozens and dozens of people. We want to find a new way, and we figured nobody knows the reasons people are leaving like our employees."

It wasn't long before the surveys started coming back. In the next two weeks, 187 of Admiral's employees returned the survey. The response was much greater than anyone had thought it would be. And what did Simon's employees tell him?

Simon started reading through the surveys one by one at 4:30 on Thursday afternoon. An hour later, he stopped and sat back. A smile crossed his face. "It's so obvious—and yet we didn't see it," he said to himself.

The Initiative

The number one reason people didn't stay at Admiral: transportation. Not money. Not benefits. Transportation. The resounding reason that the surveys cited was difficulties created by lack of transportation.

"We never would have worked this out on our own, Greg," Simon said. "And the reason is because we take our cars for granted as part of our everyday lives.

"They don't live near where they work. Many don't have cars or even a driver's license, and they're often working at hours when public transportation is either not available or just too dangerous. Would you want to stand around waiting for a bus in some parts of town?" Simon explained to a disbelieving Greg.

"It's never what you think it would be," Greg exclaimed. "I thought they'd just say 'money.' "

Simon smiled. "Don't get me wrong, they'd like more money, too. But the transportation dilemma was mentioned twice as often as financial compensation."

"Okay, so what do we do now?" Greg asked. "You're not suggesting we buy them all cars, are you?"

Simon ignored the sarcasm and explained, "My team has thrown around a few ideas, including coordinating a carpooling system, but it's too unpredictable. What we need to do is put together a shuttle system to bus our employees from their neighborhoods to the job sites."

Greg just looked at him for a moment. "You've gone too far now, Simon. You're either on drugs or you *need* to be on drugs."

"You said you wanted to solve the turnover problem, Greg. You can throw more money at them, but money won't have a real impact. If you're serious about tackling this turnover issue, transportation is the one thing that will impact this situation the most. The employees have told us that. Now we can do something about it, and in the process, win their trust and increase morale, which are bound to have an impact on efficiency and productivity. Or we can ignore what they've told us and the problem will continue to perpetuate itself."

"I'm scared to ask the next question," Greg commented.

"Then don't ask it," Simon said, interrupting. "It's the wrong question anyway. The question is not, how much is this going to cost us? The question is, how much is this going to *save* us? Depending on who you listen to, the cost of turnover is anywhere from 25 to 150 percent of an employee's annual compensation. In the case of a manager or executive, the estimate ranges from 100 to 225 percent. This means, based on our current payroll, turnover is conservatively costing us two million dollars a year. That's almost $170,000 a month, or $40,000 a week!"

Greg just glared at him, but Simon wasn't finished.

"I asked my team to work up a couple of scenarios and price them out, and I think we can pilot a shuttle bus program for between twelve and fifteen thousand dollars a month, and I think it will decrease turnover by at least 20 percent. Do the math, Greg. Give it three months. By then you'll know. In fact, you'll probably know long before then."

"All right," Greg agreed reluctantly, "but if you're wrong . . ."

Simon cut him off again. "No more threats, Greg, because the truth is, I'm miserable the way things are. If we can't get at this turnover issue, you won't have to fire me—I'll quit."

The following week, the shuttle bus system was announced. Three weeks later, it was fully operational. During the day, Admiral would bus employees to and from certain locations in four key neighborhoods, and at night they would bus them to and from their homes.

The results were almost immediate.

Attitude Shift

The first change was a new attitude among the employees. The managers pointed it out to Greg and Simon at the weekly managers' meeting.

"You have no idea how grateful some of these people are. Every day is a struggle for some of them. They want to work, they need to work, but for so long, they've believed that everyone's against them, including us," announced Brad, one of the four regional managers.

"I have to agree," said Juan, another of the regional managers. "It's a simple thing, but it has made their difficult lives just a little bit easier and they appreciate that. The fact that, as a company, we've bothered to try to understand part of their struggle really means something to them."

Not all of Admiral's employees were using the bus system, much less than half, in fact, but a powerful message had been sent.

In a very real and practical way, the lives of many Admiral employees had been touched, and Greg and Simon started to notice a change in the attitude of employees when they were asked to do something. There was a new spirit of cooperation . . . you could see the adversarial spirit dissolving . . .

One Year Later . . .

Over the next year, employee turnover fell from around 400 percent to 224 percent. It had been a tough year, and turnover was still a serious problem and a top priority at Admiral, but real progress had been made. A record profit had been posted, and Simon and Greg both knew that the reduced turnover was the biggest contributing factor. And the other factors were all derivatives of having addressed the turnover crisis.

It was also interesting to note that sick days were down 31 percent from the previous year, and lateness had been reduced by 65 percent. The managers noted at their quarterly off-site review how much pressure this had taken off them and their teams.

Simon left a report outlining these results on Greg's desk, and left the office.

As he drove home that night, Simon had a genuine feeling of satisfaction. He knew he had not solved the problem entirely and he was still having to hire far too many people. But he knew he had begun something revolutionary, and that gave him a deep sense of fulfillment.

The next morning, Greg came into Simon's office with a bonus.

"I want you to know I doubted you at every turn, but the survey and the shuttle bus ideas were great. I actually see the reduced stress among people. It's more enjoyable for me to come to work, and even though at times I can be rude and impatient, I want you to know that I am grateful."

Simon could hardly believe his ears. It took a moment for him to shift into that gear with Greg, and by the time he did, it was over.

"I need you to do another survey!" Greg barked.

Simon just about fell off his chair. "You hate my surveys."

"I know. I know. But that was in the past. I hated your surveys when they were costing me money. Now they're making me money. Find out what's next on the list," Greg said.

"What list?" Simon asked, toying with him a little.

"The 'Why people leave Admiral' list!" Greg insisted. "And hire another assistant. You're going to need one. We are going to get to the bottom of this turnover thing and build an extraordinary team."

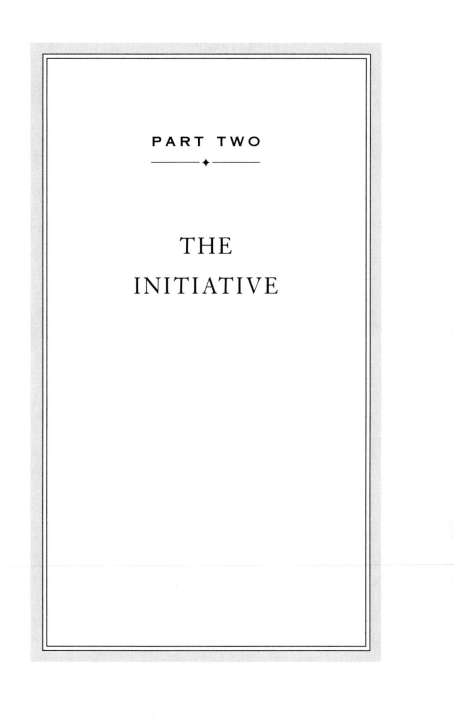

PART TWO

THE

INITIATIVE

The Obvious

Simon was determined not to lose the momentum. He called an executive meeting to ask the question . . . again.

"We have made great strides, but we still have work to do if we're going to beat this turnover thing," Simon announced to his executive team. "I think we have to ask the question again. Why do so many people leave Admiral?"

Most just shrugged their shoulders and said, "If we could pay them more, they would stay."

Sometimes, when you get too close to something, you can't see it for what it really is.

When Sandra starting talking, every head in the room swiveled in her direction, and several of the team looked at her as if to say, "Who is this and why is she speaking?"

Sandra Anderson was Simon's new assistant and he had asked her to sit in on the meeting with him. Not easily intimidated, she spoke up, saying, "The problem is, they don't see any future in it."

Everybody in the room knew that. It was the obvious answer. But the leadership team had become immune to it. It had been overlooked because they believed they couldn't change it.

"Come on," said Jeff, Admiral's operations manager, "let's get honest with ourselves. It's a dead-end job. You know it and they know it."

"But does it have to be?" Sandra asked, baiting him.

Peter was the manager of region one, the team that cleans the stadiums and concert venues, and he came to Jeff's defense now.

"I think Jeff is right. We're not going to get around this one. Cleaning toilets, vacuuming offices, and picking up trash in stadiums is always going to be a dead-end job, isn't it? I mean, we might want to believe otherwise, but it is what it is. It isn't like people dream about being a janitor when they're in high school."

"I think you're wrong!" said Sandra. It may have been her first week, but Sandra wasn't afraid to speak up, maybe *because* it was her first week. Simon felt the muscles all over his body tighten. He feared Greg would just devour her with one of his moments—Greg was famous for them. He would throw things and scream. But he surprised Simon . . . again . . . by patiently asking, "What do you mean, Sandra?"

She cleared her throat and said, "Well, it could be a dead-end job, or we could make it a stepping-stone."

"A stepping-stone to what?" Jeff asked sarcastically, and a couple of the other managers snickered among themselves.

"Say more about that, Sandra," Greg pressed.

"These people all have dreams. We need to find a way to connect their job today with their dreams for tomorrow. I've been studying the turnover reports all week, and it seems that on average we keep an employee for about six months. A year ago, the average was three months. Imagine if we could increase that to three years. That alone would radically transform our whole business model."

"She's right," interjected Simon. "Unless we can link their job here and now with their richly imagined futures, the turnover issue will plague us forever."

"Will you listen to yourself," said Jeff. "Dreams and richly imagined futures. These people are unskilled labor. They don't have richly imagined futures."

"Then we need to help them with that, too," Simon volleyed.

"These jobs are dead-end jobs. People don't dream of being janitors. It is what it is. We can't change that!" exclaimed Jeff. Around the table, heads were nodding in agreement.

"I think we can," Simon persisted. "I think we can help our employees build a bridge between their NOW and a better FUTURE. Dreams are the bridge. We need to convince them that this is not a dead-end job, and the only way to do that is to demonstrate that working here can help them get where they want to go."

Dreams Drive Us

Nothing was resolved when the meeting came to an end, and Greg made a mental note that Jeff seemed pleased with that.

Simon trudged back to his office a little deflated. The past year had been filled with great progress, and that had been both fulfilling and exciting. But he knew he was up against another brick wall. This time it wasn't with Greg—it was with the team.

He slumped into his chair and turned toward the window.

"What are you thinking?" Greg asked, poking his head into Simon's office.

"Does it ever occur to you to knock before you enter someone's office?" Simon asked.

"Not really," Greg said, grinning.

"Lots of things. I'm thinking lots of things," Simon said, and then paused.

"Tell me about them. I'm in an unusually patient mood and find myself predisposed to listening, which as you know is even rarer than my patience."

Greg sat down and Simon began to speak.

"If you ask people to talk about their jobs, they usually reply with a rote answer or a sales pitch that they've given a thousand times before, unless they are really doing something that they're passionate about. But if you ask people to talk about their dreams, in most cases you'll see a remarkable increase in their passion and energy."

"So what are you saying?" Greg asked.

"I think Sandra is on to something here . . . Dreams drive

us! We have to find a way to make a connection between people's daily work and their dreams," Simon explained.

"What do you mean?" Greg asked, looking for a little more clarity.

"If we can help our employees beyond the quiet desperation of mere survival by teaching them to dream again, and help them to fulfill their dreams, we'll create a loyalty and dedication that's unmatched. And then our people will bring the passion and energy they have for their dreams to their work."

For several long minutes, Greg just sat there in silence, pondering all that Simon had said.

"Think about it like this," Simon continued. "How important are your dreams to you?"

"Very important," Greg conceded.

"Don't your dreams drive you?"

"Of course they do. I've been chasing down dreams my whole life. If I don't have a dream to chase, I am miserable. Dreams motivate me to get out of bed in the morning and make something of my life," Greg replied.

"Exactly. So what makes you think that your employees' dreams are any less important . . . or powerful?"

People

The next morning, when Simon arrived at work, Greg was sitting in his office.

"I couldn't concentrate at the show last night, and you know that's your fault."

"What's wrong?" Simon asked.

"Simon, I think you're on to something here, and that scares me and excites me all at the same time. I've asked Sandra to cancel your morning meetings. I think we should talk a little more about people and their dreams."

Simon smiled. His relationship with Greg had always been very transactional. Greg told him what needed to be done, and Simon either did it or saw to it that someone else did it. He wasn't used to the new relaxed and reflective Greg, but he liked him and hoped he'd stick around.

"So, talk to me about what you're discovering or realizing about people," Greg said.

"I think we've forgotten that people are people," Simon began. "At Wal-Mart they call them 'associates,' at McDonald's they call them 'crew members,' at Starbucks they are 'partners,' at Disney they call them 'cast members,' here at Admiral we call them 'team members,' and at most places they just get called 'employees' or 'staff.' But in all of this, we've forgotten that first and foremost they're people." He could tell that Greg was really interested and listening, so he continued.

"What sets people apart? People are unique in that they have the ability to imagine a more abundant future, to hope for that future, and to take proactive steps to create that future. This is the process of proactive dreaming. Isn't that the story of all great individuals, families, teams, corporations, and nations?"

Simon paused for a moment to take a drink of water before going on.

"In many ways, we *are* our dreams. But people stop dreaming because they get caught up in the hustle and bustle of surviving.

And once we stop dreaming, we start to lead lives of quiet desperation, and little by little the passion and energy begin to disappear from our lives."

"You've got me inspired," Greg said, "but I don't see how this translates into the business environment, or how it fixes our turnover problem, or even if it's our job to help our employees fulfill their dreams."

"I'm not 100 percent sure myself yet," Simon admitted, "but I do know that if we can make the connection between our employees' daily work and their dreams for the future, we will unleash an energy that will transform our business. And while it may be argued that it's not our responsibility to help our employees fulfill their dreams, I would pose the question: Isn't one of the primary responsibilities of all relationships to help each other fulfill our dreams?"

Greg and Simon sat talking for hours until Sandra couldn't hold off the employees any longer. Questions needed to be answered, phone calls returned, and meetings rescheduled . . . and everybody was wondering and whispering about what Simon and Greg had been talking about all this time.

Sleepless Night

Later that night, Simon lay awake in bed, thinking about his conversation with Greg. As he lay there watching his wife, Melanie, sleep, his own words kept coming back to him over and over again: "Isn't one of the primary responsibilities of all relationships to help each other fulfill our dreams?"

It gave him pause to think that he didn't really know what Melanie's dreams were at this time in her life.

When they had first met and started dating, they had talked about their dreams, and Melanie's dream had been to get married and raise a family. But their children had been out of the home for several years now.

I wonder what her dreams are now? Simon thought to himself.

Next month, they would be married for twenty-five years, and it pained him to think they had not had an explicit conversation about their dreams in all that time. They had talked about things they wanted to do, and made day-to-day decisions about the direction of their lives and those of their family members, but they hadn't really talked about their dreams.

Simon lay there watching her sleep, her chest rising and falling, and her chestnut hair flowing over the pillow. This was the woman he loved—but what were her dreams?

And now, an even graver thought crossed his restless mind. He began to wonder, *How many of her dreams have been lost along the way while I was too busy pursuing my own?*

His heart sank and his eyes welled with tears.

When Melanie woke, it was morning, and Simon was still lying there watching her. He hadn't slept all night, and now that she was awake he took her in his arms and held her. They lay there tangled up in each other for a long time, and began to talk about their dreams for the future.

Then they spent the morning writing a list of things they would like to do, places they would like to see, things they would like to have, relationships they would like to focus on . . . and all the dreams they could find in their hearts.

They took an inventory of their dreams and made a promise to each other that, from now on, they would pay closer attention to them. They knew they had a long way to go, but they had taken the first step.

Making the Connection

It was this exercise with Melanie that led Simon to his next step at Admiral. The following week, with Sandra's help, he put together another survey.

They called it the "Dream Survey." It was specifically designed to develop an understanding of the employees and their dreams.

"We've asked them about our business, and we've asked them why they think people leave Admiral. Now we need to know what drives our employees," Simon explained to Greg and the rest of Admiral's leadership.

"Money," piped up one of the area managers.

"You may be right, but I suspect we'll find it is much more involved than that," Simon replied.

The Dream Survey had only one question: "What are your dreams?"

It got some strange looks, and comments, but by now the first survey was famous, even legendary. The employees who had been there for the first survey needed no convincing that they should participate openly and honestly in the Dream Survey.

They knew from the previous survey that Simon and his team wouldn't ignore their responses.

When the surveys started coming back, it became clear very quickly that Admiral's employees had dreams. Simon and Sandra spent the next couple of weeks working through the surveys, reviewing employees' individual dreams, and looking for common dreams.

The variety of dreams people described in their responses was extraordinary and eye-opening. Simon realized that things he took for granted every day were distant dreams that others only wished and hoped for. And it quickly dawned on him that the executive team, and many of the managers, had no idea what drove the people they managed and worked with.

Some wanted to go to college, others wanted their children to go to college. Some wanted a car, others a vacation. One employee simply wrote, "a proper Christmas," while another wrote, "a better life for my children." Some wanted to learn English, others wanted to teach Spanish, and more than a few dreamt of owning their own business.

What was the most common dream among the employee responses?

Home ownership.

More than 60 percent of those who turned in their surveys included the desire to own a home as one of their dreams.

Astounding, Simon thought to himself.

It was at that precise moment that Greg walked through the door. "So what do you think?"

"These people have got dreams, Greg, and in many ways they're simple dreams . . . and you know what, they deserve a chance to accomplish their dreams. And from the perspective of self-interest, if we can help some of these people achieve even just one of their dreams, we'll create an unimaginable base of goodwill and loyalty," replied Simon.

It was more than Greg had bargained for, and he was sold, but he teased Simon with another question. "So how do we do it?"

Simon paused and looked up. "I don't know yet."

Genius and Madness

There is a fine line between genius and madness, and when Simon showed up at Greg's house on Saturday morning, Simon wasn't sure himself which side of that line he was on.

Greg was in his driveway, washing his car, when he saw Simon pull up. It was only the second time in five years that he had stopped by the house, so Greg immediately had a sinking feeling.

"What's wrong?" Greg called across the lawn.

"Nothing," replied Simon. "I hope you don't mind me stopping by, but I think I've worked it out."

"Worked what out?" Greg said, toying with him a little.

"I know how to do it now, to make the connection between people's dreams and their work."

"Go on . . ." pressed Greg.

"We need a Dream Manager!" Simon announced.

Greg cocked his head. "Excuse me?"

"We need a Dream Manager," Simon repeated.

"Who or what is that?" Greg asked, in a tone that wavered between curiosity and sarcasm.

"A Dream Manager is someone who will help our employees achieve their dreams," explained Simon.

"How will this Dream Manager do that? And, even if I did agree to this insanity, where would we find ourselves a Dream Manager?"

"The Dream Manager will meet with employees, discuss their dreams, and help them put together a plan to achieve their dreams. Once a month, they can meet with the Dream Manager, assess their progress, and discuss next steps. As for finding one, I'm thinking it should be a cross between a life coach and a financial advisor, because most dreams involve a financial component."

Greg just looked at him for a long moment, then he said to him, "Hold on. You have actually spent a lot of time thinking about this, haven't you?"

Simon just nodded.

"You're mad!" Greg barked.

"I might be, but think of the possibilities if this were to work."

"How much will it cost?" Greg asked, softening a little.

Simon knew Greg would ask the money question, so he had already done a quick cost analysis. He smiled and said, "To test the Dream Manager concept for one year will cost less than 20 percent of what you've saved in reduced turnover costs over the past twelve months. But again, the real question is, 'How much will it make you?'"

"Well, how much will it make us?" Greg urged.

"I honestly believe that, if you do this right, it will make you a fortune. I mean, I think it will double your profit margin and double the size of your business in five years. Not only that, we'll revolutionize the way people manage people forever."

Greg didn't say anything, and Simon could tell he was going to that far-off place of deep thought, so he reeled him back with a question.

"Let me ask you this, Greg. How grateful are you to the people who helped you achieve your dreams?"

"Extremely," Greg conceded.

"Wouldn't you like your employees to be that grateful toward you?"

"Of course. Wouldn't anyone?"

"Can't you see how that would change the energy, attitude, and dynamic here at Admiral?"

"Sure I can, Simon, but . . ."

"Help your employees in the direction of their dreams and you will create the most dynamic environment in corporate America!"

At that moment, the front door opened and Greg's wife glared at the two of them.

"I've got to go," said Greg, a little sheepishly. "I promised her we wouldn't be late for brunch with the kids. Let's talk more on Monday."

Boldness

Now it was Greg's turn to have a sleepless night. He got out of bed at 1 a.m., having lain there wide-eyed for two hours, and began to pace around the house. Before long, he found himself standing in front of a bookshelf in the living room. He didn't like to read, but he found himself attracted to a small yellow volume.

It turned out to be exactly the type of book he *did* like. It was a collection of quotes, *The Book of Courage*. With just one quote to a page and plenty of blank space, it made him feel it was manageable, and he began to leaf through the pages one after another.

"Don't be afraid to take a big step if one is indicated. You can't cross a chasm in two small jumps."

"He who is not courageous enough to take risks will accomplish nothing in life."

"There is nothing more powerful than an idea whose time has come."

"Be bold and mighty forces will come to your aid."

"The measure of your life will be the measure of your courage."

"When all is said and done, when you are too old to drive your cars and spend your money, when you are finally alone with nothing but your thoughts and memories: What contribution will you have made?"

Greg slowly shut the book. More than any other time in his life, he knew he was at a crossroad. He could coast along, and things would go generally the way they had gone in the past, or he could shift gears and change direction.

This is my chance, he thought to himself.

Standing up, he looked around the quiet house. The silence was eerie for a man who always had to have the radio or television on, but he felt peaceful, and that, too, was unfamiliar.

Getting back into bed, he decided that this was one of those decisions that defines a person's life.

A Bold Move

The next morning when Simon arrived to work, there was an e-mail waiting for him from Greg.

> "I'm taking the day off. Find us a Dream Manager. You are either a genius or a madman. Let's find out which it is."

In the time Simon had been at Admiral, he had never known Greg to take a day off. A smile came across his face, and behind that smile were a thousand thoughts.

Sandra walked into his office to say good morning, and, seeing the look on his face, she asked, "What are you smiling at?"

"He said yes," Simon announced, renewing his smile.

"No," Sandra retorted in disbelief.

"Yes, he did. Today, we're going to start looking for a Dream Manager. Let's get the executive team together tomorrow morning to discuss where we go from here."

Finding a Dream Manager

The next morning, as the executive team gathered around the conference table, Simon unveiled the Dream Manager Initiative. There was a genuine feeling of awe among most of the players. They knew it was revolutionary; they just didn't know if it could be pulled off.

Not everyone was impressed, of course—there were also some real detractors. But Simon had no time for them anymore. He had come to the realization that they were never going to take the business to the next level. Their negative energy said something about them, not about him or his idea. "So I called you together this morning to get your input before we begin the search for the Dream Manager," Simon announced.

Mike, head of sales for Admiral, was the first to speak up, saying, "People will be lining up for this job."

"Why do you say that?" Greg inquired.

"Think about it. How many people do you know who actually have a job where they can help people fulfill their dreams?"

"Yeah, but after six months when he realizes he can't help these people fulfill their dreams, he'll be running for the door. Dream Manager! Have you people taken your medication anytime in the last week?" griped Jeff.

"No, I think Mike is right," said Julie. "There are a lot of people who would love a job like this."

Julie was the director of marketing for Admiral. She was

one of the older people in the room, but she was not jaded or cynical, and she quickly got behind Simon on this new initiative.

"How will we choose who gets the job?" Mike asked Simon.

"I'm not sure. That's one of the reasons I wanted us all to get together."

"Well, I'd like to throw my hat in the ring," said Mike.

"That raises a great question," replied Simon. "One of the first things we need to decide is, should it be someone internal or someone external?"

"Internal," said Peter.

"Why?" three people asked at once.

"Why not? It should be one of our own. Someone who cares about Admiral and the people here," Peter replied.

"No, I disagree. I think it should be someone external," said Sandra, who now attended almost every meeting.

"Why?" the same three people asked.

"It needs to be someone outside of the politics. Someone perceived as neutral by the employees. A new entity . . ."

"Ooooo . . . an entity," teased Jeff, as full of sarcasm as ever.

"Yes, an entity," Julie said, stepping in. "Do you have any idea how much this could change some of our employees' lives? Think about it. Most people don't fail because they want to fail; they fail because they don't know how to succeed. Whether it's in relationships or with their finances, people want to succeed. The Dream Manager will help them find a way. And if that is not an entity, then I don't know what is. It needs to be someone new and fresh, someone from the outside who can bring an aura with them to the position."

"I think you are right," agreed Peter, and a consensus of nods shuttled around the room.

"How will this solve the turnover problem?" Jeff asked.

"I'm glad you asked." Simon beamed. "As best I can tell, there are two things that keep people interested in a job: the sense that they are making a difference and the sense that they are progressing or advancing. Now, we are under no illusions here at Admiral, we are a janitorial company. We are not curing cancer and we are not organizing the cancellation of Third World debt. The sense that we are making a difference is limited, so we have to give our employees an abundance of the latter. We have to give them an opportunity to progress and advance. When people feel they are progressing, they are much less likely to start looking around for another job. It is when they don't feel that they are advancing that they start to get restless."

"So will the Dream Manager offer career counseling?" Peter asked.

"Once every six months, an employee will have the option to invite his or her supervisor to their monthly Dream Session. During that session, the Dream Manager, the employee, and his or her supervisor can discuss a vision for the employee's future—but particularly, what the next career step is and how long it will take to achieve that next step," Simon explained.

"If you get these people dreaming, won't they leave us even faster? I mean, most of them are still in dead-end jobs," pressed Peter.

"No and no," Simon replied. "Many people desperately need someone to help them articulate their dreams, whether they are aware of it or not. They will stay because, for many of them, this will be the first time anyone has ever really sat with them and helped them map out a future. The whole point is that, because of the Dream Manager, the job is no longer dead-end. It becomes a stepping-stone. Even if, three years from now, they are still doing the same thing here at Admiral that they do today, they will have made enormous progress in other areas of their lives—and they will link that personal progress to their job here at Admiral. The Dream Manager Initiative will create a connection between the fulfillment of their dreams and their work."

Julie interrupted, "I think you're right. I've been thinking about something Sandra said at her first meeting. We can't keep these people in these jobs forever, but if we can convince them to work hard in a role for three years, that will be a vast improvement on our all-time low of three months . . . and that will change our entire business model."

The conversation lulled and Simon could see that people were starting to really think about the impact this new initiative could have on Admiral's business and environment.

"Internal or external?" Brad asked, refocusing the discussion.

Simon called for a show of hands for each.

"External it is, then," he announced. "I'll let you know when we have found a suitable candidate and what the protocol will be."

The Arrival

The following week, Simon interviewed twenty-seven people for the position. Sandra had placed advertisements in all the local job-hunting outlets and the applications had been flowing in.

Sean Evans was the candidate that Simon and Sandra finally agreed to present to Greg as their number one choice. He had a degree in business, had been working as a financial advisor for nine years, had a history of drive and excellence, and his community involvement suggested he was interested in helping people. Noticeably, he had also grown up in a tough part of town, and that made Simon think he might understand the plight of some of the employees at the lower end of the totem pole.

Greg took Sean to lunch after a brief get-together with Simon and Sandra. When he returned, Greg announced that he agreed that Sean was the man for the job.

Over the next three weeks, all the arrangements were made for the Dream Manager's arrival. In the meantime, Simon and Sean were meeting off-site every day for a couple of hours to discuss more clearly the roles and responsibilities of the Dream Manager. When Sean was not with Simon, he was reading over the Dream Surveys, and he was learning a lot about the dreams and drives of the employees.

Back at Admiral's headquarters, Sandra had been preparing Sean's new office.

Everything about the office was different. It didn't look like any other office at Admiral, and that was intentional. The furniture was inviting and warm, there were couches, and in many ways, it was more like a living room than an office.

But the first thing Sandra did was arrange to have a sign made and hung on the door: THE DREAM MANAGER. The sign had been on the door for almost three weeks before Sean arrived . . . and the anticipation had been growing steadily.

Skeptical, Cynical, Resistant

Jeff was a nice enough guy. He was married with a couple of children and had been in management for about fifteen years. By most people's standards, he had a really good life. But he was always the critic. He was resistant, cynical, skeptical, and generally resentful of enthusiasm and new ideas.

"When did you stop dreaming?" Simon asked him quietly one morning when Jeff stopped by with a vacation request form that he wanted expedited for one of his team.

"What do you mean?"

"Well, I noticed that you didn't return your Dream Survey."

"I thought they could be anonymous?" Jeff said, on guard now.

"That's true, but yesterday when I was in your office, I saw one in your trash can. I guess I assumed it was yours."

Jeff looked angered. A moment passed and Simon just stood there, calmly, in the silence.

"I guess I'm just content," Jeff said uncomfortably.

"For someone who is so content, you seem to have a lot of pent-up frustrations. I think you're settling in some area of your life, maybe more than one, and I've been trying to figure out when and why you stopped dreaming."

"You don't know what you're talking about," Jeff said defensively.

"Maybe you're right," Simon conceded, "but I think you have just been coasting along here, and in life, for some time now. You're surviving, but I don't think you're thriving. And I think it's because, somewhere along the way, you stopped dreaming."

Jeff just looked at him, stared for a moment, and then, again very defensively, said, "I'm just content. Not many people are."

"I think that's a cop-out," volleyed Simon.

Later that night, Jeff was sitting quietly at home thinking about Simon's question, "When did you stop dreaming?" He just couldn't seem to put it out of his mind. At some deep place within him, he knew Simon was right. As a young man, it seemed, he'd had so many dreams, but he couldn't pinpoint the moment when that all started to slip away. So he came to the conclusion that there had not been any one moment when he'd stopped dreaming. It had happened so gradually that he hadn't even noticed it until Simon had asked the question.

Who's First?

For a couple of weeks, people had been casually stopping by Sean's office just to chat and check him out, but it was time to get the formal process going. The question that needed to be answered was, "Who would be first to have the chance to meet with the Dream Manager?"

"Who should we start with?" Sean asked the executive team.

"Those who need it the most," said Peter.

"No, no, no. Our best people should go first," Greg suggested with some force.

"But they don't need it," Peter argued.

"That may be true, but those who need it most need to see that it can work. We have to build confidence in the Dream Manager Initiative," explained Simon.

"I think that's right," agreed Julie. "Once the employees see a couple of people accomplishing dreams, they will be more passionate about their own dreams and the Dream Manager process."

"Absolutely, so we need to find some A-level employees with some large but achievable dreams and we need to put them on the fast track to fulfilling those dreams," concluded Simon.

"So who wants to be first from the executive team?" Sean asked.

They just looked at each other. The truth is, they had never really thought of the Dream Manager Initiative as something for them. They had convinced themselves that they could be their own Dream Managers. This program wasn't something they needed; it was something people lower down on the totem pole needed. At least, that was what they had told themselves.

Sean could tell from the looks on their faces what they were thinking. When the silence had lasted long enough and no-body had replied, he continued, "The Dream Manager Initiative has to be for people from all levels of the organization, not just those at the labor level, but management, administration, and executives."

"This is not for us, this is for the janitors," Mike said.

"I think you're wrong," Sean replied.

"But they're the ones who need it."

"We all need it. Taking this job has made me see that I need a Dream Manager, too. Everyone needs a Dream Manager. To a certain extent, we can do it for ourselves. But we all need someone who can help us articulate our dreams, determine the priority of our dreams, pull together a plan for the fulfillment of those dreams, and hold us accountable on a regular basis for the actions that help us achieve our dreams or hold us back from our dreams," argued Sean.

The temperature in the room was rising and a passionate discussion was emerging. The back-and-forth went on for another ten minutes and Greg leaned back in his chair and smiled to himself. He was so pleased because he could not remember the last time his team had had a real, honest-to-goodness argument in a way that was healthy. Nobody was attacking anybody personally; it was a genuine sharing of opinions, a debate over ideas, a healthy conflict in search of the best way.

Finally, Sean said, "We have to start with natural and hierarchical leaders. Both are necessary if this thing is going to succeed. For some of you, this is going to require a level of humility and vulnerability that you're not used to. But if you open yourself up to it, these two qualities will help you in your work, in your relationships, and in your quest to accomplish your dreams."

By talking it through, an unspoken agreement had been reached. There was no need to take a show of hands. The consensus was evident.

The whole room was in shock when Jeff said, "I'll go first!"

Jeff had been the biggest critic of the Dream Manager Initiative and everyone knew it, but Simon's question had been hounding him for a few weeks now.

"When can I come by?" Jeff asked Sean, to break the disbelief in the air.

"How about first thing tomorrow morning?"

The First Session

The next morning, Jeff was in Sean's office when he arrived just before 8:00 a.m. In Jeff's hand was a crumpled list of his dreams. Simon had seen it in his trash can and had rescued it just after their conversation.

Sean was pleased that Jeff had chosen to get involved, but he was also a little nervous.

"So, what's your dream?" he asked Jeff, to break the ice.

"As it turns out, I have lots of them."

"You seem surprised by that," Sean commented.

"I am. You see, in the beginning, when Simon first started talking about this whole Dream Manager thing, I thought he was crazy. But then he took me aside a couple of weeks back and said something that pierced me. He made me realize that I had stopped dreaming."

"Why did you stop dreaming?" Sean asked.

"I've been trying to figure that out. Maybe I just slowly began to subscribe to the idea that we live, we work, we pay our bills, raise our children, and then we retire. Or maybe I stopped dreaming because I was afraid I couldn't achieve my dreams. I don't really know."

"And now?"

"Well, now I see it differently. I've started dreaming again. I just sat out on the deck one Saturday afternoon and quickly began to realize that there are places I want to go, and things I want to see, and relationships I want to improve. And I see that many of my dreams are achievable. But most of all, there are things about myself that I really don't like, and I want to change them."

"Wow!" whispered Sean. He wasn't sure if he even meant to say it aloud, but he was genuinely in awe of Jeff's honesty. "Let's start by going through your Dream List and just talking about them."

One by one, Jeff read his dreams to Sean and explained why each was important to him. Then Sean asked him, "Okay, so which of these would you like to achieve in the next six months?"

Jeff was silent for a moment and Sean purposefully let him think. He didn't intrude on his reflection, and he didn't force Jeff to an answer.

"I think I'd like to do the trip to California. I've always wanted to drive across the country . . . and I would really like to work on being a more positive person."

"Great. Now tell me, do you have any vacation time saved up?" Sean asked.

"That's the thing, I have nine weeks of vacation set aside, and I've been thinking to myself, *Set aside for what?* My wife is always telling me that if I took regular vacations I wouldn't be so highly strung, I'd enjoy life a little more, and then I would be more positive. Maybe what I need is a vacation."

"Fantastic. What about finances for the trip?"

"Well, I was thinking I could travel for three weeks, and I've got money saved, but I was thinking I should set some money aside from each paycheck for the next four months. That way, I'll be motivated to save more and I'll have something to look forward to," explained Jeff.

"Great. Let's take the time to write out a plan so that next month, when we get together, we can review it. You also need to give some thought to who will cover your role while you're gone."

Jeff and Sean then looked at some numbers and wrote out a plan, both financial and practical, for the accomplishment of Jeff's first dream. After that, they talked about the ways Jeff thought he could become more positive.

"Well, I think you are already becoming a more positive person. I've sat in on five meetings with you since I got here and you were more positive today than in any of the others, so you just have to keep it going. Remember—try to stay focused on progress, not perfection. Sometimes when we think of how far we still have to go, we get discouraged."

"Thank you," Jeff said.

"Oh, you're very welcome," Sean replied. "I really want to

tell you how impressed I am with the way you've been willing to open yourself up to this process. You've made yourself vulnerable, and I know that hasn't been easy."

Jeff was a big guy and had a reputation for being a tough man to deal with. Clearly, something was happening in his life and Sean was excited to be a part of it.

"When's our next get-together?" Jeff asked, to divert attention away from the compliment.

"One month from today at 10 a.m."

"Perfect!" Jeff exclaimed with a smile.

"It would be helpful if you could go through your Dream List between now and then and put an estimated time frame on each of your dreams. Don't be unrealistic, but don't be too soft on yourself. The secret is to stretch yourself, but not so much that you break," Sean explained.

The first Dream Session was over and Sean felt pretty good about how it had gone, but not as good as Jeff felt. Jeff could already feel a new energy and excitement within himself.

The Dream Manager Initiative was in motion.

Financially Illiterate

Each of the regional managers had compiled a list of employees whom they thought should be among the first invited to a consultation with the Dream Manager. Sean had asked them to do this and had then followed up with each of the employees during the month since his first meeting with Jeff.

He was sitting at his desk when he heard a knock on the door.

"Come in," he called.

Greg opened the door and walked in. Someone had finally taught him to knock. Sean had laid down the law and explained that he couldn't just be walking in on people's Dream Sessions.

"How's it going?" Greg asked Sean.

"I've got to tell you, you're really doing something extraordinary for your employees, Greg. They appreciate it, and I really believe that you're going to see benefits you had not even calculated."

"I hope so, it's costing me a fortune. So, tell me, what are you seeing? I know you can't talk about people's specific dreams, but what have you discovered in general through the process?" Greg asked Sean.

"The most disturbing thing to me has been the amount of financial illiteracy. I thought it would exist among the lower-paid employees, but it's amazing how prevalent it is even among the managers."

"Say more about that," Greg coaxed.

"Mark Twain once wrote, 'Those who don't read great books are at no advantage over those who cannot read.' The same is true when it comes to money. Those who don't manage their money well are no better off than those who don't have money to manage. There are a lot of people here making really decent incomes who are still financially unfit. There are people here whose job it is to manage budgets or various accounting functions, who don't have a budget themselves, cannot or do not balance their checkbooks, and are laden with consumer debt."

"Can we help them?"

"Absolutely," Sean explained. "That's my specialty, in fact, and one of the main distractions in people's lives is money worries. When people are worrying about money, it can be all-consuming and it affects their work. One by one, we'll introduce them to the laws of money and help each of them create a plan suitable to their income and their dreams. The truth is, most people have never really been taught the laws of money."

Rita

Nobody was more excited than Rita to meet with the Dream Manager.

Rita was a fifty-four-year-old woman with a good heart and a strong mind. Her dream, for as long as she could remember, had been to own a home. As Rita looked back over her family history, she could not find a single person who had owned the home they lived in. Her parents had rented, her grandparents had rented, and her great-grandparents had rented.

Rita's was a common dream, and Sean quickly identified her as a leader.

"This is a huge opportunity. If we can help this woman to live her dream, it will get the attention of an awful lot of people here at Admiral," Sean said to Simon.

"Can she afford a house?"

"That's the thing. I've been talking to my friend Dan, who is in the low-cost housing business, and he says there are some great ways to get this woman in a new house. It will be in a neighborhood much better than the one she's in now with no money down, and her mortgage payment will be only sixty dollars more than she is paying in rent. Plus, her interest payments are tax-deductible, she'll be paying down the principal each month, and the property will appreciate."

In their second meeting together, Sean and Rita did a financial survey, developed a debt assessment, and put together a savings plan.

"You are going to own a home before you know it, Rita," Sean declared.

Rita beamed. When she had left Sean's office, he called Dan to set up a lunch meeting. They had been friends since childhood. Dan was an entrepreneur, in the classical sense of the word, a property guru with a larger-than-life personality and an attitude that anything was possible.

When Sean had first mentioned the Dream Manager Initiative, Dan had been fascinated. Later, when he'd described Rita's situation and dream, Dan became intrigued. Dan had enough money for ten lifetimes. He still loved the thrill of a deal, but the only thing that really satisfied him these days was helping other people.

At lunch later that week, Dan agreed to help, and told Sean that he would have his people start scouting for houses.

Simon's Friend

When Greg walked into Simon's office, Simon had his feet up on the desk and his eyes closed.

"Sorry to wake you," Greg said, announcing his presence. Simon wiped his eyes, but Greg couldn't tell if he had actually been sleeping.

"What are you doing?" he asked Simon.

"Dreaming!"

"Nice. Is that what I pay you for?" quipped Greg.

"Actually, yes," Simon said with a smile. "I was reading a story the other day about Henry Ford giving some guests a tour of his factory and offices. As they passed one door, there was a man with his feet up on his desk and his eyes closed. The guests asked Mr. Ford why he didn't seem to mind that this man was sleeping on the job. Ford replied that he wasn't sleeping, he was dreaming. 'Doesn't that bother you?' they asked Ford. He replied, 'No. He is just doing his job. You see, that man invented the six-cylinder motor and disc brakes. His job is to dream up things that my competitors think are impossible.'"

"Well, I'm sorry to interrupt your dreaming. I just came by to see how things are going with the Dream Manager Initiative," Greg said.

"Things are great," Simon replied. "Jeff is taking his road trip across the country in a couple of weeks, Susan from accounting just got a new car with Sean's help, Michael is taking his wife on a cruise for their anniversary, thanks to the Dream

Manager Program, and I am fairly confident Rita will be in a new house within six months."

"And what about turnover?" asked Greg.

"I haven't seen the latest numbers Sandra has been putting together, but I know it is still falling. At any rate, I have to run. I have a lunch meeting. I'll stop by with the numbers after lunch and we can talk more about it."

Simon's lunch was with a friend from business school. They'd been in the habit of getting together once a month for lunch, just to catch up and bounce ideas off each other, but they had not met for about nine months. Ed was a banker, a regional manager in charge of Ohio, Indiana, and Kentucky.

"So what's happening at work?" Simon asked Ed, even though he already knew the answer.

"We just can't get this turnover monkey off our backs. I was at a national meeting of all the regional directors last month and our president identified the reduction of turnover as one of three major strategic objectives . . . and our greatest challenge over the next five years!" Ed explained.

"Your competitors must have the same problem, though?" Simon asked.

"Sure they do, but that's no consolation. The truth is, turnover is just draining profits. Last year, turnover costs for the bank were equal to 30 percent of annual profits. How's the turnover situation at Admiral? I know you have it much worse than we do."

"Not anymore," Simon said and smiled. Ed could tell by the look on Simon's face that he knew something that he wasn't letting on to.

"What do you mean, 'Not anymore'?" Ed asked, playing along.

"We've reduced turnover by 50 percent in the past year and it's still falling."

For the next half hour, Simon explained the surveys, the shuttle bus system, and the evolution and implementation of the Dream Manager Initiative. Ed just sat there listening with amazement. But as Simon went on, he noticed he was starting to lose Ed. "What's wrong?" he asked him.

"That might work for janitors, but it won't work for bankers," Ed said, sounding discouraged.

"Why, bankers don't have dreams?" Simon nudged.

"Sure they do, but . . ." Ed stammered.

"But what? Your people have dreams just like my people. They may have different dreams, but they have dreams! You're not at a disadvantage; you're at an advantage. Think about it. Not only will it work for your employees, but they can also become Dream Managers for your customers. The first question our Dream Manager asks an employee when he sits down for a Dream Session is, 'What's your dream?'"

Ed looked at him. Simon was a man impassioned, a very different man than he had been last time they were together.

Simon continued, "This is the question your tellers should be asking every time a customer comes into the bank: 'What's your dream?' The customers may not say anything, but they will start to think about the question."

Ed now stared in amazement.

"In time, you could provide Dream Managers for your best customers. Imagine the loyalty that would imbue in them. And as I think about it, in many ways, you already do. Those financial advisors you have are ripe to be transformed into Dream Managers. Let's face it, the reason most people want to manage their money is so they can achieve their dreams. Dreams drive us. If you help your employees identify their dreams and pursue their dreams, they will do the same for your customers, and your business will boom."

After lunch Ed went back to his office, closed the door, and sat there in a daze. Later that day, he called Simon to offer him a job at the bank, launching their Dream Manager Initiative.

Simon declined, but explained that he would be happy to meet with his leadership team, explain the idea, and give Ed some guidance on hiring the right Dream Manager. Simon also mentioned that he would be willing to have Ed's leadership team visit with Sean and some of the employees at Admiral to talk about the process.

"What are you doing next Thursday?" Ed asked.

"Living the dream!" Simon replied, with a huge smile on his face. He couldn't think of himself as a genius, but he knew that the pendulum was swinging away from the madman end of the scale. For the first time in many years, Simon consciously became aware that he felt good about who he was, where he was, and what he was doing.

English Classes

Sean was using some of his time between appointments to pore over the Dream Surveys that Simon and Sandra had conducted before his arrival. He had read through them once when Simon had first offered him the job, to get a sense of what he was getting himself into, but now he was studying them in a more systematic way.

Home ownership had been identified as a common dream early on in the process, but he wanted to go beyond that now.

More than 65 percent of Admiral's employees had minority backgrounds, and 50 percent overall were Hispanic. Many didn't speak English, and all supervisors had to be bilingual. It was a prerequisite.

One of the most common dreams among the Hispanic employees was to learn English.

Sean contacted the local community college and arranged for one of the professors to come in and teach English twice a week. Between the afternoon shift and the evening shift, employees could sign up for English classes that would be taught at headquarters.

The response was overwhelming.

After three weeks, Sean had to find an additional teacher, and they added two extra classes. After six weeks, at the request of the employees, they allowed the employees' children to start attending the classes also. Many of the employees were first generation Americans, and their children were struggling in school because English was a second language in the home.

Then, one afternoon when Sean was sitting in his office, there was a knock on the door. It was Rob, one of the area managers. He wanted to volunteer to teach one of the English classes and suggested perhaps one of the other employees could offer a Spanish class for any Admiral employees who wanted to learn or improve their Spanish.

"I like the idea, but there could be problems," Sean explained. "If we have supervisors being taught by their direct reports, it might not sit well with some."

"I've thought about that, Sean. But how do you think a janitor will feel if you give him the opportunity to teach his peers and managers his own language. If you are serious about building a team, this could be one of the largest steps you take in that direction."

"It will take humility," said Sean.

"Exactly," Rob agreed, "but that humility will breed unity and dissolve the 'us versus them' mentality faster and more effectively than any speech or corporate memo ever could."

"All right, let's give it a try. I will need your help finding a couple of the bilingual employees willing to teach Spanish," Sean concluded.

Check-up

The weeks passed and each day Sean was filled with a greater sense of satisfaction. He'd never imagined that his professional life could change so radically at this stage in his career. In some ways, he was doing what he had been doing as a financial advisor for the past nine years. Only now, the scope of his work was broader, his approach was focused on the employees' dreams rather than the sale of products, and, most of all, there was a rare openness and willingness among the employees to make themselves vulnerable.

Every day, he met with employees to discuss their dreams and the strategy they had mapped out together in earlier sessions. He had also been meeting with Simon's friend, Ed, and his colleagues at the bank. Just that very morning, he had received an invitation from the National Association of Financial Planners to speak about the Dream Manager Initiative at their national convention later that year.

Simon had been there for Sean but had always tried to keep himself at arm's length in order to ensure the integrity of the process. He wanted to give Sean the autonomy he needed to build confidence and thrive as the Dream Manager. But on this particular day, he had scheduled a meeting with Sean just to check in and see how things were going.

"What has surprised you the most?" Simon asked, to begin.

"I guess I am continually surprised by how much this whole process has changed me and my life. I was hired to help transform the employees' lives, but I find they are transforming my life," Sean replied.

"Tell me more about that," Simon said, inviting Sean to expand.

Sean fidgeted with some papers on the desk in front of him. "Well, let me give you two examples. The first is that I think I have been dreaming a dream that was programmed into me for most of my life. My dreams have been challenging, but they have never really taken me out of my comfort zone. Now, I am starting to dream dreams that take me outside that comfort zone and that is both frightening and exhilarating."

"What's the second example?" Simon inquired.

"My relationship with my wife. I've come to realize how attentive to and supportive of my dreams she has been over the years, and how inattentive I've been to her dreams. We've started talking about her dreams and I see this whole part of her that's been trapped or caged for so long. She wants to start a small business, so we've decided she is going to quit her job, take a part-time job, and start her business part-time. We've restructured our budget and we'll have to tighten our belts a little at first, but it's a dream of hers and, more than ever, I feel like she deserves a shot at that."

Simon smiled. Not so long ago, he had felt that quiet desperation that Thoreau had written about, but now he felt a deep and quiet satisfaction.

"And the work with the employees, how's that going?" Simon asked.

"Terrific. I have to tell you, Simon, it's humbling. To have these people sit there and open their hearts and their lives to me is powerful and humbling. But I must say, it makes me feel responsible."

"Is there anything I can help with?"

"There was one thing I wanted to run past you," Sean said, and paused before going on. "A lot of these people need legal counsel of one sort or another. They're little things, mostly, but it's outside of my expertise, and I'm spending a lot of time researching different things. I'd like to contact one of the local firms and see if they would provide an attorney pro bono, or at a reduced rate, for three or four hours once a month, to talk through some of these things with our employees. What do you think?"

"Great idea. Give Steve Jacobson a call, over at Burke and White, and see if they can tie it into their community service program. Tell him who you are and that you work with me. They may be able to help us."

Day to Day

The days and the weeks passed and Sean kept meeting one-on-one with the employees. Each session opened his eyes more and more to the dreams people kept hidden away in their hearts.

His days got busier and busier. There seemed to be an insatiable appetite for the Dream Manager Sessions.

It continued to amaze him on a daily basis how just talking about our dreams starts to move us in the direction of them. He noticed that the employees were being transformed before his very eyes. They still had all the problems they'd had just a few short months ago, but now they had hope.

The hope came from having a plan. Sadly, in many cases, nobody had ever taken the time to sit with these people and help them formulate a plan.

At the request of several employees, Sean had started allowing spouses to join them for their Dream Sessions, and this provided some surprising new developments and benefits. The spouses were blown away. Most of them worked for other companies, and so they knew the Dream Manager Initiative was unique.

Daniel's wife was a perfect example. Daniel was twenty-seven and had been with Admiral, working as a janitor, for four years now. His wife, Rachel, worked for a hospital downtown. Daniel had been meeting with Sean for almost six months before he asked Sean if he could bring his wife to his next Dream Session.

At the end of his first meeting with Daniel and Rachel together, Sean asked her, "So what do you think?"

"It's amazing," she replied, and Sean could tell she was in a bit of a daze.

"What do you mean?" he probed.

"Well, I've been sitting here for the last thirty minutes, listening to this little voice in my head ask me questions like: *How concerned do you think your manager is about your career? What about your employer? Do they care about your personal development?* And the answer is, they don't. Or if they do, they haven't bothered to share it with me. What you are doing for Daniel, and me, and your other employees, is powerful . . . and I just want you to know that I am really, really grateful."

Rachel stopped, but Sean could tell she had more to say. After a long moment, she continued, with tears welling in her eyes. "Daniel is a new man. It has been amazing to witness the passion and energy he has lately. It's made him a better husband and father, and I'm sure a better employee. For the first time since we dated, we are dreaming together again, and not just talking about the future but building a future together.

I can't tell you how much this has begun to change our lives and how good it is to wake up next to a man who has dreams to chase."

Sean's days were filled with stories like these, and over and over again he tried to affirm Simon and Greg on the bold move they had made in starting the Dream Manager Program.

Sean felt privileged to be able to do what he did.

The House

Simon had known from the beginning that it was important to help some employees achieve some big dreams. He knew some early success stories were pivotal to the overall success of the program, because he knew the quicker some dreams were accomplished, the more Admiral's employees would get involved in the Dream Manager Program.

He had conveyed this to Sean, who had taken it on board and made Simon's sense of urgency his own.

With that in mind, Sean had focused on helping Rita find and buy a house. He was with her at every step in the process, and now it was going to become a reality. In the first few months, there had been several dreams accomplished, but this would be the first big dream to be realized.

Sean had arranged to go with Rita for the closing at the bank, and then Simon and Sandra had joined him to take Rita to her new home. As they drove into the driveway, Sean said, "Well, now it's yours!"

Rita was next to him in the front seat, beaming.

"I just don't know how to thank you," she said. "I'm fifty-four years old and, until 132 days ago, nobody had ever asked me what my dreams were. Nobody!" Her gratitude was palpable, and Simon, Sean, and Sandra had a sense of accomplishment that words could not describe.

One hundred and thirty-two days after her first meeting with the Dream Manager, Rita was in her new home. She had been counting the days. With no money down and a monthly payment just slightly higher than her rent, Rita moved into the first home her family had ever owned.

You would have been hard-pressed to convince anybody that there was a happier woman on the planet. Rita became a living, breathing advertisement for the Dream Manager Program.

"If you are not seeing the Dream Manager, you need your head read," one of the managers heard Rita saying to one of the younger women. To one of the young men on her team she said, "That's right, you keep talking like you're a victim, but the truth is you still haven't put your name on the list to see the Dream Manager . . . so you've got no one to blame but yourself. You either don't have dreams or you're scared of your dreams! You know which one my money is on!"

Word about Rita's house spread like wildfire through the company. Everyone was talking about it, and Rita wanted everyone to see it.

Rita was on fire about her house, about Admiral, and about life. Greg couldn't remember the last time he had felt this good about himself, and life, and the company. He never imagined his work would have this much meaning. For more than twenty years, he had resigned himself to the idea that his work was work, a kind of work that people would rather not be doing, and he just had to make the best of it. But now everything was different.

Greg started spending an hour each day visiting the sites and talking casually to his employees about their dreams and the Dream Manager Program in general. Listening to their dreams, he realized two things: how many people, things, and opportunities he took for granted in his life, and how critical it is that managers know the dreams of the people who work for them.

Rita had her home . . . and dreams began to flow like rivers at Admiral.

Greg's Response

The executive team was assembled and waiting for Greg to arrive when someone said to Jeff, "So, you never really told us, how was your trip?"

"Amazing! Just to drive across America and see all the different places was extraordinary, but to have that time with Samantha was really a new beginning."

Everyone just looked at him. Most of them had noticed a change in his attitude, but now it was there before their very eyes for all to see. The one who had once been the most skeptical, cynical, resistant member of the team was now speaking openly and honestly about his newfound enthusiasm for life.

"I have to tell you," Jeff continued, "I was very skeptical of this whole Dream Manager idea from the beginning, but after my trip, I just feel like a different person."

"So what's next?" Simon asked him.

"Well, Samantha has always wanted to go to Paris. So Sean has helped us put together a savings plan, and we are hoping to spend a couple of weeks in France next summer," Jeff said with a smile.

At that moment, Greg walked in, but as he often did, he started speaking before he had entered the room.

"So what do we have?"

The team launched into the agenda, and after about thirty-five minutes, Simon announced the last item.

"The last item is a review of the Dream Manager Program."

Sean reported to the team, though his reports seemed hardly necessary anymore. Any news that he had to bring to the table had already traveled several times around the corporate offices at Admiral.

"I say we get everyone a house," Greg announced.

"That's not the answer," Simon said in response.

"Well, why not?" Greg asked, a little deflated.

"Because everyone has different dreams," Simon explained.

"He's right," Sean added. "One of the first principles Simon taught me was that as a Dream Manager you always have to remember that every person has different dreams, and that you cannot force your dreams on another person. Think about how much damage is caused when parents try to force their dreams on their children, or when one spouse tries to force his or her dreams on the other."

"That's the truth," exclaimed Mike loudly.

Everyone looked at him. There was something behind his comment. It had a sting to it, and there was an awkward silence.

"Sorry. It's just that all this talk about dreams has had me reanalyzing my relationship with my ex-wife. What I am coming to realize is that she was always trying to force her dreams on me, and I was always trying to force my dreams on her," he explained.

"It's amazing how much this stuff applies to our everyday lives, isn't it?" Brad said. "I've been thinking about my dating life. I have dated some wonderful women, but it never lasts. Then, yesterday, it dawned on me that I never got interested in their dreams. I couldn't even tell you what their dreams were, and you know what else? I never shared my dreams with them. So we were together, but we were apart, because the way I see it, it's impossible to have a great relationship without sharing your dreams."

Brad had discovered a whole new turnover problem and had found that the same solution applied. Dreams bring us to life. Dreams animate us, and what dreams do for individuals, they also do for relationships . . . and companies. The pursuit of dreams creates passion, energy, enthusiasm, and vitality.

The team went on talking for some time about how different people's dreams really are. Peter talked about how his teenage son's dream was getting his driver's license. Julie spoke about how her husband had been dreaming about taking an Alaskan cruise for as long as she had known him.

"So, last Wednesday, when he mentioned it, I said to him, 'How much longer are you going to just go on talking about that?' On Thursday, at lunch, he went to the travel agent to get some brochures, and yesterday, he booked the trip. I wish I had challenged him ten years ago."

Greg told the group that his wife had decided to go back to college, that that was her dream. Sean explained how he had been spending more time with his father, because one of his dreams had always been to have a better relationship with him. "I just decided I wasn't going to wait for him to make the first move anymore, and it has been really special."

It was becoming very clear to everyone that one of the most powerful dynamics in relationships is trying to understand the other person's dreams, and helping them chase and fulfill those dreams.

"What I'm realizing is that we are all Dream Managers," Lauren announced to the team. There was an air of stunned amazement in the room—not because of what Lauren had said, but because she never spoke at meetings unless called upon.

Lauren was Admiral's CFO and was one of those quiet and meticulous personalities. She continued, "If we really want to help people, we have a responsibility to help them identify and pursue their dreams. In that way, I'm a Dream Manager for my husband, for my children, for my friends, for my colleagues here, and for people who just pass through my life. Not in the same way Sean is a Dream Manager, but every relationship improves when we are mindful of each other's dreams."

The Gatherings

One night, as Greg was leaving the office, he overheard his assistant saying, "Are you going to Rita's tonight?" He asked her, "Is Rita having a party?"

Rita had started having a gathering in her house every Tuesday night for family and friends and anyone from Admiral who wanted to come. It had been going on for a few weeks now.

Everyone would sit around and visit while they drank coffee and ate cake, and then Rita would tell her story.

Like everything else, word of these gatherings had spread throughout Admiral and people were falling over themselves to get there now. Everyone had heard about Rita's house, but now they wanted to see it for themselves.

And seeing was believing.

The way Rita told her story about her dream, the Dream Manager, and all Admiral had done for her, she could have sold those people anything. Over the next six months, more than 60 percent of her fellow workers came to one of her gatherings, and once again, the power of authentic leadership was displayed.

This woman, a janitor, almost single-handedly converted the remaining unbelievers at Admiral. Her enthusiasm for the Dream Manager Program was contagious.

Word quickly got around town as well, and it wasn't long before the press started calling. The *Business Courier* did a story that discussed the new program Admiral had initiated and focused particularly on Rita and her new house.

The following week, Simon had seventeen job offers. He turned all of them down.

The Stampede

Now the door to the Dream Manager's office was being beaten down. Simon, Sean, and Greg started receiving letters from employees complaining that it was taking too long to get their first appointment with the Dream Manager.

At this point, less than 50 percent of the employees were participating in the program, but that still meant 150 meetings a month for Sean.

Sean came to Simon to announce the inevitable: "We need another Dream Manager."

"I think you're right. Do you want to do the search, or would you like me to?"

"If you could do it, that would be great. I'm swamped as it is," Sean said, more than a little relieved that he didn't have to add that to his workload.

Over the next couple of weeks, Simon was able to come up with three candidates, all of whom he thought could easily fill the role. But he wanted Sean, Sandra, and Greg to weigh in on the decision, so he arranged for all three candidates to have one more interview and they all sat in on it.

After the last candidate left, Simon turned to the others and asked, "So, what do you think?"

"I agree, they're all great," said Sandra.

"Me, too," said Greg.

"Yep. Any of them could do the job and do it very, very well," confirmed Sean.

"I sense a 'but' in there, Sean," Simon probed.

"I think it should be Michelle," he explained.

Michelle Watkins was a successful forty-two-year-old corporate trainer who also had a small life-coaching business, and never thought she'd be applying for a job at a janitorial company.

"Why her?" Sandra and Greg volleyed.

"I didn't know it myself at the beginning, but there's a psychology to being a Dream Manager. You have to focus on encouraging people and giving people permission to pursue their dreams. You have to avoid judgment, and provide tools and accountability, but you can't take responsibility for them achieving their dreams."

"Why do you think Michelle would be better than the others?" Simon asked.

Sean explained, "She's had experience with these things. Her work as a corporate trainer has taught her how to facilitate rather than dictate. Great facilitators draw the answers out of the audience, rather than imposing the answers upon them— and that's perfect for this. On top of that, her experience as a life coach is invaluable. It's like she's been training for this job for the last ten years."

The team was convinced and they hired Michelle the next day. Admiral had its second Dream Manager.

Appreciated

From time to time, Greg would stop by Simon's office just to chat. There were two things that were different about these visits. The first was that Greg always knocked now and, even if the door was open, he waited to be acknowledged before entering Simon's office. The second was that he no longer stood and prowled back and forth like a tiger as they talked. These days, he took a seat on the small couch and got comfortable.

One thing had not changed. Greg always had an agenda.

"Do you think this thing can be duplicated?"

"What thing?" Simon teased.

"The Dream Manager Program," Greg said.

"Absolutely. As you know, I have helped some of my friends in banking and insurance start their own programs regionally, and I think, within the next twelve months, both of those programs will go national," Simon explained.

"Is there resistance among these people when you explain the program to them?" Greg asked.

"Always."

"And why do you think there is such resistance?"

"Two reasons. First, because people are always looking for quick fixes and there are no quick fixes to situations that involve real, living, breathing people. The second reason is that too many businesspeople believe business is only about making money, so they can't think beyond the paradigm that wants to use money to solve problems."

"Tell me more about that," Greg said.

Simon could tell Greg was trying to get to something, so he kept talking. "It's a bit like something I learned many years ago when I was in college. I was dating a girl who was working for an incentive travel company and I asked her, 'Why don't these companies just give their employees the money as a bonus?' She explained that if they hand over the money, employees tend to use it to pay off their credit cards or to buy a new television—which is nice, but doesn't have the same impact as a trip. If they give employees the trip, they get a break from their work, they associate the excitement of the trip with their work, and they feel rewarded for their work, all of which encourages them to work hard again in the year ahead. On top of all that, they tell their friends about the trip, their friends will think it's great, maybe even be a little envious, and all of this makes employees feel good about the company they work for."

Greg looked thoughtful, so Simon went on. "The employee-employer money paradigm is a thing of the past. The modern employee is looking for things much more abstract than a simple pay raise. Sure, they want to be well compensated, but they are conscious of lifestyle, work environment, and more than ever they want work that is engaging. So when I explain the program to other managers and business owners, their resistance is natural, because they are operating from the old paradigm that assumes that people come to work just to make money. To some extent it may be true, but in most cases, people don't come to work *just* to make money, and the more money they make, the less it becomes about the money."

Simon began to sense that he was losing Greg, so he coaxed him back by saying, "Let's face it, Greg, your first reaction was to throw money at it. You wanted to give them a pay raise, hoping that would fix the turnover problem."

"You're right, you're right. But let me ask you this, if it's not just about the money, what is it about?"

"Money is certainly a factor, and, for many, the biggest factor. Another factor is meaningful work, but most people don't have their sights set that high. Most employees aren't that ambitious. Many have simply given up on the possibility. For hundreds of years, the battles between employees and employers, between owners and workers, between unions and corporations have created an 'us versus them' mentality that is detrimental to the collaborative spirit of teamwork needed to succeed in business."

"So what else, besides money and meaningful work?" Greg persisted.

"Employees want to feel appreciated. Eighty-five percent of people who leave a job leave because of their relationship with their direct supervisor. And when you ask them about their relationship with their supervisor, they almost inevitably say that he or she didn't appreciate them or their contribution. The predominant concern of employees isn't money or benefits, and it's not hours. They want to feel appreciated."

"Do you think our employees feel appreciated?" Greg asked Simon.

"You better believe it. The Dream Manager Program is living proof that Admiral cares about their employees. It is proof that we care about who they are and that we appreciate the contribution they make to our enterprise. Appreciation is the strongest currency in the corporate culture."

"What do you mean?"

"Melanie is so good about letting me know that she appreciates the little things I do for her. I can't stand doing some of them, but knowing how much she appreciates it makes me feel better about doing them. A few years ago, she told me that she really appreciates the way I understand her need to spend time with her girlfriends. Three years ago . . . but it still helps me deal with that when I would rather have her all to myself. If I tell my kids that I really appreciate the way they mowed the lawn and took care of the garden without having to be asked, they feel good about themselves and chances are I won't have to ask them half as often. Nobody likes to feel that they are being taken for granted—that just builds resentment. But appreciation makes people feel good about who they are and what they are doing."

"I see it now. I used to feel that resentment among our employees. It was like poison in the air around here."

"And now?" Simon asked.

"Now I can't visit a site or bump into an employee without being thanked for something. I've got to tell you, Simon, in more than twenty years in business, I have never had an employee thank me for their job—until we started the Dream Manager Program, that is. Now a day doesn't pass without someone thanking me for his or her job. People used to scurry past me as I wandered around, and now they come bouncing up to me to tell me the latest dream that has been accomplished."

"It's that appreciation that is transforming our business. Profits continue to rise, we have more and more business, turnover continues to fall, and the one thing that I notice in my daily workload is that there are fewer complaints. There are fewer complaints from employees and fewer complaints from clients, which gives me more time to work on the strategic future of the business. There is little that people won't do if they feel genuinely appreciated."

Anyone looking at the financial statements would see that costs were down and profits were up, but they wouldn't see the remarkable transformation that was taking place at Admiral.

The Bathroom

The next day, Greg walked into the bathroom at headquarters. Stepping into one of the stalls, he closed the door and, as he did, he looked with astonishment at a message on the back of the toilet door. It was a handwritten note that read: WHAT'S YOUR DREAM?

Greg stepped into the next stall. The same handwritten message was posted on the back of that door. He went along the row, from stall to stall, and found the same message in every stall.

He walked back to his office and said to his personal assistant, "Come with me." Debra got up from her desk, not knowing what was going on. She wondered if perhaps the old Greg had returned and was going to have one of his little moments.

Greg and Debra walked down the corridor to the women's restroom. "Go in there and tell me if there is anything on the back of the toilet doors," he said.

Debra just stood there and looked at him. "Go on," he said. She didn't move.

"It says, 'What's your dream?'" she said timidly. "It's on all the doors. José cleans them every night. He asked me about a week ago if he could put them up. I thought it was a good idea, don't get angry at him."

"Angry? I'm not angry. Why would I be angry?" Greg said. "I'm delighted. Ask him to come in a little early tomorrow and see me."

When José stopped by the next day, Greg praised him for what he had done, and asked him to work with Debra to have signs made and laminated for the back of each toilet door in the building.

José beamed.

As he turned to leave, Greg called him back and asked, "What's your dream?"

"I want to own and run my own business one day," he replied with a smile.

After Two Years . . .

By the end of the second year, eleven employees were living in new homes they never thought they'd own and more than one hundred employees had fulfilled the first dream on their list.

Turnover was down from 400 percent to just over 50 percent in two years.

The profits were staggering.

Greg took Simon, Sean, Michelle, Sandra, and their spouses

to the Caribbean for an off-site strategic planning session. It was a combination of work and reward. At first, he was worried that the trip would create some resentment among other employees, but their response was the complete opposite.

"I just know this trip will help them come up with the next great idea," Sandra overheard one of her colleagues saying.

They spent five days in Antigua. The beaches were beautiful, the weather gorgeous, and the synergy among the team members and their spouses was extraordinary.

Each morning, they met for breakfast and then took the meeting to Greg's suite. The spouses went to the spa or the beach or to golf. At about two o'clock, they would break until dinner, when they would gather again to dine as a group.

Greg opened the first session by explaining how successful the Dream Manager Initiative had been and how he wanted to give some of the profits back to the employees. He further explained that he wanted to redistribute a portion of the profits in three ways: by raising wages and salaries, creating a new bonus system, and enhancing the Dream Manager Program.

On the second day, Sandra's husband and Greg's wife asked if they could sit in on the meetings. "I'm just fascinated with what Sandra tells me about the program and I'd like to learn more about it," explained Sandra's husband, Paul.

"On one condition," replied Simon, "and that is that you contribute if you see something that we don't see."

The group discussed strategic direction for the Dream Manager Initiative and, during the first three days, came out with some really great ideas about how to evolve the program. Then, just before lunch on the fourth day, time had been scheduled to decide which ideas to implement and which to set aside. But as they walked into the meeting, another notion occurred to Simon, and he kicked himself for not having thought of it earlier.

"We shouldn't decide these today," he said to the group.

"We're leaving tomorrow," Greg objected.

"I know, but the truth is, we should ask the employees how they think we should enhance the program. We can't underestimate how important it was that the employees got to have a say in the beginning. We shouldn't shut them out now. Let's keep them involved in the process."

"I was thinking the same thing," said Michelle. "I think it's time for another survey."

"Exactly," Simon said, glad that someone else had suggested it.

Sean stepped in now, saying, "We can put together a short report of the ideas we have come up with, ask the employees to comment on them and assign priority to each of them, and let them add any other ideas they have."

They had discovered what they had already known, and found it to be as true as ever. There is no substitute for involving everyone in the process.

PART THREE

EXPANSION

How's It Going?

Greg was doing a lot of wandering these days. He would walk up and down the corridors, stopping by different offices just to check in. He had fewer problems and he didn't feel the need to tightly monitor Simon or the executive team as he had in the past, so he just wandered.

For the first time, he felt like he had a business. It was finally dawning on him that for all these years he had just had a well-paying job, in the sense that, if he had gone on vacation for a month, the company would have been in a shambles when he returned. But now, if he went away for a month, he was confident that the company would not just survive, but would thrive in his absence.

And that was just what he and his wife, Mary, had decided

to do. They were planning a one-month trip to Australia next summer. Mary had always wanted to travel, but Greg had always said that he hated traveling. The truth was, he hated to leave the company unsupervised, but now he didn't feel that it needed watching over.

During one of his mid-afternoon walkabouts, Greg happened upon Simon and Michelle, just coming to the end of a meeting.

"How's it going?" he asked.

"Most rewarding work of my life," Simon said.

"We are really helping people," Michelle added. "When I tell my friends what I am doing here, they can't believe it."

"It's strange, isn't it?" Greg commented. "Our people are ordinary people, from different backgrounds, no doubt, and they have their struggles. But people need someone to help them articulate their dreams, someone to speak with openly about their dreams. It's simple stuff, but it really is powerful. I lie awake at night sometimes, thinking about my employees' dreams, and I get so excited for what's happening in their lives."

"I wish you had come to me with this idea ten years ago," Michelle said.

Greg laughed and continued, "Let me tell you: I wish Simon had come up with this Dream Manager Initiative ten years ago, too. I think of all the thousands of people who have passed through this place. I always thought they were letting me down. As it turns out, we were letting each other down, but I tend to think it was more my fault than theirs."

"Don't be too hard on yourself, Greg, we've come a long way in a couple of short years."

"You're right, Simon. A lot has changed around this place in two years and I want to keep that going. Are there any problems that you see that we need to address?" Greg asked.

"Actually, that was why Michelle and I were sitting down just now. Michelle feels that there are a couple of people on our team who don't belong here at Admiral."

"What do you mean?" Greg asked, turning to Michelle.

"Well, if we are really going to transform our entire workforce, there are some people who are going to have to change or leave. Truth be told, if they haven't changed by now, they aren't likely to. I have three people in mind and they are all gatekeepers. At the lower levels, the employees will root out the lazy ones themselves now, but at the higher levels, it's not that easy."

"Who do you have in mind, and why?" Greg asked, his interest piqued.

"Charlie, Joe, and Scott," Michelle replied.

"But they're all managers!" Greg said in surprise.

"I know, but we have at least twelve people who could replace them and do a better job," Michelle explained.

"But those guys have been here for years."

"I know that, too, and that's probably why they got promoted, but they aren't the best people for the job. Think about it—what would happen to a football team if you gave promotions based on the years you had put in? Under that guise, if you sat on the bench for enough seasons, you would get promoted to the starting lineup. Football coaches put their best team on the field and we need to do the same."

"But you just can't fire them, can you?" Greg inquired.

"That's true, but Charlie and Joe have had letters from Human Resources in the past twelve months, citing them for underperformance, failure to meet goals and objectives, and noncompliance with company policy. And Scott, in my opinion, is a bully. He blames others for problems he creates and essentially lacks what it takes to be a leader," Michelle explained.

"What do you think?" Greg asked Simon.

"I think Michelle is right, and if we don't hold them accountable or weed them out, we are sending a bad message to our good people. Furthermore, it will create three career opportunities for three of our best people, and that will bring some dreams to life."

"Okay, but we have to do it in the right way," Greg urged.

"Absolutely." Michelle resumed. "I say we send them a final written warning, explaining that any further problems in these areas will lead to termination. If they rise to the occasion, we've solved our problem. If they don't, we solve our problem, but we cannot continue to turn a blind eye to poor performance and mediocre leadership."

"Good," agreed Greg. "Let's put the plan in play."

The Latest Survey

Since getting back from the Caribbean, everybody had been asking Simon what the team had decided while they were away. Simon explained that they hadn't decided anything, only that they had come up with some new ideas for the expansion and improvement of the Dream Manager Program, and now they wanted to have the employees' input on these new ideas.

The only thing the group had set in stone while they were away was that they needed to reach full participation in the Dream Manager Program as soon as possible. At this point, only 65 percent of employees had been initiated into the program. With Sean and Michelle's workloads the way they were, it would be up to a year before the rest of the employees who wanted to participate were active in the program.

This backlog meant hiring at least one, and maybe two more Dream Managers. But they wanted the other employees' feedback on this, so the full-participation idea was included alongside their other ideas.

The surveys went out and came back in record time and with a record level of respondents. Again, employees were instructed that they could participate anonymously if they wished. However, if employees chose to include their names on the survey, they had the option of having the survey passed on to their Dream Manager.

Ninety-six percent of the respondents put their names on the survey, and 100 percent of those requested that their surveys be passed on to their Dream Manager, even though many of these respondents had still not had their first meeting with a Dream Manager.

The overwhelming majority of employees listed full participation as the number one priority of the Dream Manager Program over the next three to six months.

Greg, Simon, Sean, Michelle, and Sandra had come up with some great ideas, but they had missed something that might not have occurred to them had they spent six months in the Caribbean.

The number one request from the employees in this survey was that their children be able to meet with the Dream Manager.

"Our children need a Dream Manager," or similar phrasing, appeared on 71 percent of the surveys returned.

What was true with the first survey was also true for the latest survey: It's almost never what you think it's going to be.

Culture of Dreams

Simon and his team at Admiral were building a culture of dreams. The notice board in the employee lunchroom, which used to be splattered with the kind of mundane announcements you find on most notice boards, was now covered with photos and other evidence of dreams achieved.

Each month, when the employees came to headquarters to meet with their Dream Manager, they were encouraged to stop by and check out what was happening in the lives of other employees.

The executive team had been having a series of meetings to discuss a new bonus system.

It had been eleven quarters since the birth of the Dream Manager Program, and profits every quarter had steadily increased. Greg had been pouring money back into the program, but nowhere near as much as the profits had been increasing, and now he wanted to give back to the employees in some way.

"I don't want this to be a one-time thing," Greg said to the team. "I want us to create a structure whereby a percentage of increased profits will go to the employees every year."

"What did you have in mind?" Simon asked.

"Well, I was thinking we could do three things. First, an across-the-board pay increase for all employees. Next, I thought an annual bonus system based on company and personal performance. In this case, we could allocate a certain amount to each team or department, based on profit, and they could decide how to divide it among themselves. Finally, I would like to start a Dream Fund. A percentage of profits each quarter will go into this fund. Each employee can apply for a grant from this fund for the fulfillment of a specific dream. The managers and employees can vote to say who gets the grants. We could assign categories, perhaps $500, $1,000, and $2,500 to begin with."

The team was taken aback by the thoughtfulness Greg had put into his proposal, further evidence that he was a changing man.

When Greg had finished, Sean stood up and started clapping. One by one, the rest of the team joined him. Greg was embarrassed, but each of the people in that conference room knew that he didn't have to do this.

The Dream Bonuses and pay increases were, needless to say, a huge hit with the employees, and they provided yet another injection of enthusiasm. Anyone who thought this was going to be a passing fad was now convinced that the Dream Manager Program was here to stay.

The dreams of the employees became more and more public, and this intimacy bred an even stronger sense of team unity.

As the Dream Bonuses were awarded, the recognition stimulated other employees' imaginations and the natural progression of dreams began to set in. Those who had begun with only the smallest of dreams on their list now started to dream bigger dreams. As employees achieved some of their dreams, their confidence grew, and they added even more ambitious dreams to their Dream Lists at the monthly sessions with their Dream Manager.

The recognition inspired others to action.

Something entirely new had been created. In the past, companies had been organized around cultures of hard work, excellence, billable hours, and technology. Other companies had made their mark with cultures defined by being ruthless, cool and edgy, or relaxed and fun. Now, one company had organized around a culture of dreams, and the results were extraordinary.

All of this began to awaken the realization that in a culture where dreams come true, there is no limit to the enthusiasm you can harness or the things you can achieve.

Expansion and Growth

Business was booming for Admiral. There were more clients and more income. Turnover was down, and the falling turnover meant the cost of doing business was also falling, so profits continued to rise.

There were many advantages to lowering turnover, but most of them Simon had overlooked at the outset. He had been almost obsessed with lowering turnover because he knew it was costing the company a fortune and making his life miserable. He'd known that the recruiting and training costs produced by turnover were enormous, but it was only now that they were solving the turnover issue that the many hidden costs of a disengaged workforce became apparent.

During the third year of the Dream Manager Program, Admiral's employees took only 17 percent of the sick days they had taken during the year prior to the introduction of the program. That was an 83 percent reduction in sick leave.

Over this same period, the on-time record of the employees had improved to the point where it was almost not worth measuring. Lateness was no longer an issue.

In the past, not only had there been a problem with employee turnover, but there had also been a turnover problem with clients. Not anymore. Admiral had not lost a single client in twelve months.

"It's scary, isn't it?" Simon said to Greg. "There are so many ways an employee can negatively affect the bottom line, everything from taking a sick day when they're not sick to using postage stamps for personal use."

"It's true, but if you spend too much time thinking about that, you'll drive yourself mad. Trust me, I know! I used to do just that. The thing that strikes me is that if you take care of your people, they will take care of you. For sure, there will always be some who will take advantage of the situation, but they're the ones who lose out in the end," Greg responded.

"I was thinking the same thing the other day. We have 557 employees now and our workload has increased 32 percent since this time last year, but we have used less cleaning product and materials this year than last year."

"No, it's not possible," Greg protested.

"Yes it is, Greg. I couldn't believe it when I looked at the numbers. I thought it was an accounting error, so I followed up on it. Cindy from Accounting told me that the managers have really been asking the workers to be conscientious about using products sparingly without compromising the quality of their work," Simon explained.

"Productivity is up. Costs are down. Who would have thought that these would be the benefits of teaching our employees to dream a little?" Greg said, shaking his head.

"You think that's impressive, listen to this. José, who now manages one of the commercial teams, came to me last week and said they could handle an extra building each week if we needed them to. This group has already increased their workload by 27 percent this year, and they're coming to us saying they can do more work. Let me tell you, Greg, we have created a lean, mean machine. In all my years working for you, and for others, I've had a lot of employees ask me for more money, but I have never had anyone ask me for more work."

Greg smiled.

"Incidentally," Simon continued, "José was who we chose to replace Scott after he and the others resigned a couple of months ago."

Even with the voluntary expansion of workloads, Admiral still needed more employees. Simon's focus was back on hiring, only now he wasn't just looking to fill places. He didn't have to frantically go looking for new employees and place endless advertisements on Web sites and in newspapers anymore. People were coming to Admiral now.

Admiral had been used to spending thousands of dollars and hundreds of hours painfully recruiting people, but not anymore. Now all of this resource was added to the savings created by the Dream Manager Initiative and, more positively, used toward building a more dynamic business and team.

Awards

In June of that same year, Greg was honored as Entrepreneur of the Year in the State of Ohio, and was entered into the national competition.

The national award ceremony was held at Caesar's Palace in Las Vegas and all fifty nominees were there, along with their guests, friends, and family—three thousand people in all. To help him celebrate, Greg took thirty-four of Admiral's employees with him to Vegas. Each of the seventeen teams and departments was allowed to elect two representatives to make the trip.

In his speech, Greg acknowledged Simon as the bold and brilliant mind behind the Dream Manager Initiative and spoke about how he had watched the dreams of so many people, from so many different backgrounds and so many different pay scales, come to fruition.

You could have heard a pin drop.

"So to finish, let me just say this. We all have dreams. The earlier we start dreaming, and the more mentors and friends we have who urge us on toward our dreams, the richer our lives become. In time, we learn to help others achieve their dreams, and so the cycle continues. Many of the people who work for Admiral come from a background of poverty. What I have realized over the past three or four years is that poverty is not about money. The real poverty is the poverty of opportunities. At Admiral, we believe in dreams, and we give people the opportunity to live their dreams! We set out to solve a very specific problem and instead we discovered the essence of life. What's your dream, and why aren't you living it?"

The crowd rose to their feet and clapped and cheered, and thirty-four Admiral employees could not have been prouder.

A week before Christmas, Admiral was voted the Most Admired Company in the city. Who would have imagined? A janitorial company was walking away with an honor usually awarded to some chic advertising agency or multinational corporation.

More than ever, Greg, Simon, Sean, and the rest of the Dream Managers were being inundated with requests to do media interviews, and a day never passed when a headhunter didn't call someone on the team and ask them to start the Dream Manager Program at another company.

But nobody did interviews, and nobody left Admiral.

Christmas

On the first Dream Survey, someone had written, "a proper Christmas." The survey had been submitted anonymously, but ever since Sean had read it, he had wondered who had written it.

"What a simple dream," he had thought to himself.

About six weeks before Christmas, Bob Baker came in for his first Dream Session with Sean. He was the one who had written this simple dream on the original survey, and he had written it again on the Dream List he handed to Sean at the beginning of their discussion.

Bob was twenty-three years old and had been abandoned by his family when he was fifteen. He was married with two children—Joshua, who was five, and Lisa, who was two.

It had taken him a long time to send in a request to see a Dream Manager. He was among the last of the original employees to sign up for the program, but he was here now.

Sean looked down the list of dreams and was stunned by the simplicity of the dreams Bob had written. After all his time as a Dream Manager, he had realized that there is an evolution to the way we dream. In the beginning, we choose small dreams, realize them, and then move on to bigger dreams. Sean could tell from Bob's list that he had never had much of a chance to pursue dreams, and he suspected that this was not out of laziness, but rather because he had spent all of his time and energy just trying to survive.

Any of the dreams would have sufficed as a first step, but as it was six weeks before Christmas, Sean immediately focused on that simple phrase—a proper Christmas.

"What does this proper Christmas look like?" he asked casually.

Bob began to describe it in detail. It became clear that as a child this had been Bob's dream for himself, but now it was a dream he held in his heart for his children.

As Bob described his dream, Sean wrote it down in as much detail as possible, and then they set to work writing up a plan. They did a quick assessment of Bob's financial situation and then designed a savings plan for the next six weeks.

"Three paychecks between now and Christmas. It might not be exactly what you have dreamt of for you and your family, but I am certain we can make this the best Christmas you have ever had," Sean said to Bob as he left his office.

He had set Bob to work on one plan. Sean had another plan in mind also, though he knew both were necessary to help Bob grow.

Later that day, Sean sent a memo to each of the managers and department heads, explaining the dream that had crossed his path that day. He gave the ages and interests of Bob's wife and children and invited anyone who was able to contribute to the fulfillment of this dream to send their contribution in food, gifts, or cash to Sean or Michelle's office by December 21.

December 22 was Bob's second Dream Session. It had been scheduled for December 12, but Sean had purposefully canceled and rescheduled. When Bob arrived, Sean sat him down and asked him how the plan they had put together had worked out. Bob had stuck to the plan conscientiously and had saved diligently.

"It's like you said, Sean, it won't be all I dream of and I won't be able to make my entire credit card payment this month, but it will be the best Christmas we've ever had."

Sean smiled and stood up. "I'm so proud of you, Bob. Let's take a walk."

They walked down to a spare office where the administrative staff had been piling the gifts for six weeks. Just before they reached the office, Sean told Bob that he had shared his dream with some of the other employees and they wanted to help out.

At that moment, Sean opened the door and Bob could not believe what he saw. It was a mountain of generosity. Basketballs and baseball bats, a dollhouse, running shoes and a bicycle, clothes and an iPod, and food and candy enough for a Christmas feast.

He turned to Sean and said, "Ah, man. You are so good."

Everybody Sells

Petra worked for Admiral cleaning office buildings in the downtown area on the overnight shift. Her uncle managed a building on Fifth Street and at their family Christmas party she said to him, "Uncle Joe, why don't you let us clean your building? You know we'll do a better job."

In March, when the contract was up for renewal, her uncle Joe had Admiral bid on the job. On the first of June, they started taking care of his building.

"I heard we got the contract for old man Lindner's building on Fifth Street," Greg called down the hall to Simon.

Simon got up and walked down to his office.

"It's true, but did you hear how we got the contract?" Simon replied.

When Greg heard the story, he called over to Accounting

and had them cut a check for one thousand dollars. On his way home, he drove by the building where Petra was working, thanked her, and gave her the check.

Again, word spread through Admiral like wildfire, and now everyone on the payroll was looking for new business for Admiral.

Admiral's sales force went from three rainmakers to an army of more than 550 salespeople overnight. Everywhere they went, employees were looking for new business.

And the business experienced another explosion.

"It just makes sense if you really stop and think about it," Greg explained to the executive team. "Most businesses fail because they have a few rainmakers and an army of administrative support. In any successful business, everybody has to be part of the sales force. When everybody sells, you're destined to succeed."

The atmosphere in the room for these executive meetings was now one of camaraderie. Some of the team members wouldn't have chosen one another as friends in a social setting, but that created a necessary diversity. That diversity gave birth to dynamic collaboration.

What they had always wanted to believe was now before their eyes to be witnessed and experienced. Once people know you care about them, that you are invested in them, they respond in kind, and then everybody sells.

Let's Be Realistic

At the beginning of their next meeting, Greg announced that no employee had left Admiral in ninety days, marking an all-time company record.

"Well, I think it's time for some people to leave," said Simon.

"Excuse me?" Greg replied in shock.

"I think some people need to move on from Admiral," Simon repeated.

"What are you talking about?" Greg asked, clearly a little bit agitated.

"Nobody wants to clean offices and toilets forever. Some of these people have been working hard taking different courses, some of them are even taking college classes. If they can't move up in the organization, we should help them move on to another place where they can continue to advance and fulfill their dreams," Simon said, explaining himself.

"Are you crazy? First we're trying to keep them and now we're trying to help them leave?" Greg argued.

"He could be right," Peter interjected. "If we don't, they'll begin to disengage and before too long we'll have all the same problems we used to have . . . underperformance, lateness, sick days, laziness, turnover."

"Peter's right," said Simon now. "We can't hold them back. Some turnover is good. Zero turnover isn't healthy. If we elevate them and help them achieve their dreams, some of them are naturally going to outgrow us . . ."

"Hold on," Greg interrupted. "Even if I did agree to this madness, how would you make it happen? You can't just throw these people out and say, 'Sorry, you outgrew us.'"

"No, it wouldn't be like that at all," Simon explained. "What we need is another Dream Manager, a different kind of Dream Manager, with a background in recruitment or placement. This Dream Manager would be in charge of finding our employees positions outside of Admiral if and when they outgrow us."

"You mean like an internal placement agency?" asked Greg.

"Exactly."

"You're crazy. You are absolutely nuts. Our objective here was to get people to stay. Now you want me to facilitate their departure?"

"Yes," Simon said, a little sheepishly.

"Let me make sure I've got this right," Greg said. "You want me to hire someone to get our employees jobs elsewhere."

"It's good for our business, Greg," Simon pleaded. "This may be perceived as a step beyond self-interest, but it isn't. This is what's best for the business."

Greg just glared, and Simon continued.

"This will win the respect of your employees on a level that most employers would never even dare to dream of. People will see Admiral as a place where dreams can be accomplished, a place where they won't get stuck forever. People who want to achieve their dreams will want to come and work here. So we will keep attracting the right type of people. People who are hungry and willing to work hard to achieve their dreams."

"All right, all right," Greg said, as if it was all too painful to hear. "I know you're right. It's just that we've worked so hard to build a team here, and these people feel like family now."

"And they are like family, but sometimes you have to let go," Simon concluded.

The team came to a consensus and arrangements were made to find a new member for the Dream Manager team. This person would help Admiral's best and brightest employees broaden their horizons and go off in pursuit of their dreams.

Simon had managed to convince Greg and the others that turnover wasn't always a bad thing. Some people needed to be encouraged to move on because they were toxic and poisonous to the team. Some simply were not a good fit. But others needed to be encouraged to move on because they simply outgrew the organization.

Zero turnover should never be the goal.

High-Class Problems

"Times have changed, Greg," Simon said, as he passed by Greg's office.

"How so?" Greg asked, as Simon came in and sat down.

"Last week we advertised three positions and got seven hundred applications. Seventy-five percent of them were related to or referred by our employees," Simon explained.

"I know. This morning, I was speaking to Sean and he told me that at the end of almost every Dream Session, the employee asks him if there are any jobs available. They say, 'I've got a brother . . . an aunt . . . a friend . . . ' "

This is a good problem to have, Greg thought to himself. He could remember the not-so-good old days.

Simon continued, "Yeah, you know Sean has come up with a name for this specific type of problem."

"What is it?"

"He calls them high-class problems."

"I like that. Some people have real problems. Just ask our competition," Greg said with his signature grin.

Consulting

After almost four years of resisting, Simon had finally decided to do some consulting around the Dream Manager concept and principles. Greg had agreed to let him have one day a week off to work as a consultant with other companies. So Simon teamed up with a couple of old friends in Chicago to launch a consulting company.

His first client was the bank his friend Ed worked for. They piloted a test program in the Ohio, Kentucky, and Indiana region for six months. It was phenomenally successful, so they launched a Dream Manager Program for the bank's best customers . . . and their business in the region exploded.

Simon wasn't doing it for the money. He wanted to know for himself, and prove to others, that the idea had merit beyond the janitorial industry.

Over the next twelve months, he helped a bank, a fast-food

chain, an insurance company, and a hotel chain all address and begin to tame their massive teamwork and turnover problems.

As he suspected, people in every industry have dreams.

The Competition

Sandra overheard a conversation in the lunchroom between three of the employees. "Regency called me and offered me a job. They said they would give me a pay raise."

"So what did you tell them?"

"Well, I talked it over with my wife and she said to me, 'So, you go over there and they give you a few extra dollars, but where will it get you? The people at Admiral really care about you and your future. Does Regency have a Dream Manager?' I knew she was right, so I told the people at Regency I was going to have to pass on their very generous offer."

"The Dream Manager Program creates loyalty," Sandra explained to Michelle, "and in any industry where there is a growing shortage of labor, it is the ultimate competitive advantage."

What Does It Cost?

Days and weeks and months passed and the Dream Manager team grew and grew. When the company reached 625 employees early in the fourth year of the Dream Manager Initiative, Admiral hired its eighth and ninth Dream Managers.

At one of the team meetings, one of the new DMs, Brian,

said, "I was out to dinner with a college friend and his wife over the weekend. He still works for the bank I was with before I came to Admiral, and he asked me straight out, 'How much does it cost?' I really didn't know the answer. Does anybody? I mean, do we know how much the Dream Manager Program costs?"

Simon smiled.

"What are you smiling at?" Brian asked.

"Greg asked me the same question when I first came to him with the idea, and it's the first question the companies I consult for ask me, too. Tell your friend he is asking the wrong question."

"What's the right question?"

"In the beginning, I told Greg the right question was: How much will it save? But over time, that question evolved into: How much will it make? And now I think it's important to ask: How much will it cost if they *don't* implement the program? Because the truth is, we thought we knew the cost of turnover. Experts and consultants had told us it was anywhere between 25 percent and 100 percent of an employee's annual compensation. We knew it was more than that, but we didn't know how much more. Just last week, I read that research conducted by Bliss & Associates reveals the cost of turnover is at least 150 percent of an employee's base salary."

Brian looked at Simon, starry-eyed.

"So, you go back and tell your friend that he's asking all the wrong questions. In fact, the real question isn't even: How much does the Dream Manager Initiative save in turnover costs? The real question is this: How much would you be willing to spend to create a highly efficient, cohesive, and enthusiastic team that cared about your business, if you knew that every dollar you spent would come back to you threefold or sixfold or tenfold?"

Brian smiled and Simon continued, "And one more thing—tell him if he wants to keep pumping you for information, he should hire you as a consultant or make a contribution to your favorite charity."

The team loved being in the midst of this kind of energy.

"Listen up, people!" Simon continued, addressing the whole group now. "Over the next twenty years, there is going to be a war over labor and talent in this country. *BusinessWeek* reports that over the next ten years, 21 percent of top management and 24 percent of middle management positions across all functions, regions, and industries will become vacant. In the areas of unskilled labor, we all know that the statistics are much harsher and the shortages more drastic."

These were ideas he should have been sharing with America's corporate leaders, but he was sitting around a conference room with some key employees of a janitorial company.

"Some of you will outgrow Admiral. That's okay. While you're here, keep your eyes and ears open and learn as much as you can about the Dream Manager Program, and when the time comes, take it somewhere that needs it. To think of Admiral as only a janitorial services company would be a mistake. We're in the business of helping people achieve their dreams; janitorial services is just the vehicle we use to provide that opportunity. Businesses are rarely what they appear to be, but make no mistake—dreams are the currency of the future."

The Unspoken Need

"What do people need?" Simon drilled his team of Dream Managers.

"Meaningful work," one replied.

"Or?" Simon asked.

"The sense that they are progressing and advancing," another offered.

"Or?"

"The belief that they are moving toward the fulfillment of their dreams," a third team member added.

"And what is your job?"

"To help people articulate their dreams."

"And?"

"Assist them in formulating a plan for the achievement of short-term, medium-term, and long-term goals."

"How do you know if it's a good plan?" Simon continued his questioning.

"It has to be manageable and measurable, and at the same time it needs to stretch them."

"Why is a plan important?"

Nobody answered. The DMs who had been there longer knew the answer but wanted the newer DMs to work it out.

"Open your Dream Manuals to page seventy-six," Simon said, raising his voice just for effect. Sean and Michelle had put together a Dream Manual that outlined the process for the employees. "What does it say?"

"Those who fail to plan can plan to fail," they replied in unison.

"Why do we do what we do?" Simon asked now.

Alex, one of the new guys, said, " 'Cause I'm a good guy!" and the room chuckled.

"Wrong, but thanks for playing. Why do we do what we do?" Simon continued.

Michelle spoke up now, saying, "Because people spend most of their lives working, so they should enjoy it, or at the very least know that it is moving them in the direction of their dreams."

The Invisible Power of Dreams

Up until now, everyone at Admiral had resisted the temptation to do interviews with the media. They had published some of their notes and manuals on a public Web site to help other companies who wanted to emulate the program, but they didn't feel media coverage was necessary. And then came the call that seemed too good to turn down.

Sandra had been promoted to Dream Manager about twelve months earlier, and she had hired Stuart as Simon's new assistant. It was Stuart who had taken the call.

At the time, Simon had asked not to be disturbed and had his phone blocked accordingly. So when Stuart went into his office, Simon had his eyes closed and his feet up on the desk.

"Sorry to interrupt, but I think you'll want to take this call," Stuart explained.

"Probably not," Simon replied, without even opening his eyes.

"It's Linda Gray, the producer of *The Frank Morgan Show*."

"And?"

"They want to know if you'll appear on the show."

Simon still didn't open his eyes or take his feet off the desk. "Tell them I'm flattered by the offer, but no thank you."

Stuart just looked at him.

"Is there a reason you're still standing in my office?" Simon said a few minutes later, sensing that he was still in the room.

Stuart went back to his desk and picked up the phone. The voice on the other end of the phone was clearly used to getting a very different kind of response.

The next afternoon, Stuart received another call for Simon; this time it was Frank Morgan.

"You can't not take this one," Stuart said to him. "It would be rude, even arrogant."

"Hello!" Simon said, picking up the phone.

The conversation that followed consisted of Simon turning down the request again and Frank Morgan arguing that millions of Americans would benefit and be inspired by the wisdom Simon had discovered and was now in a position to share in an interview.

The following Tuesday, Simon appeared on *The Frank Morgan Show*. It was one of those rare moments in television when the person being interviewed was not selling something and was undeniably interesting just because of who he was and what he had accomplished.

"How did this idea of a Dream Manager ever come to you?" Frank asked to begin.

"You know, we had a big problem and it seemed every other company was just trying to put a Band-Aid on the problem, and I started to think that we needed a radically different solution. Looking around at our employees, they just seemed miserable. So I started to ask myself: How can we inspire these people? And we're a janitorial company, so I knew it wasn't going to be the work. Then I thought about all the gimmicky things corporations do in an attempt to inspire their employees. And then I started to study the very nature of inspiration and observe what people are most inspired about. It was then that I discovered that we are driven by our dreams."

"In what way?" Frank asked, intrigued with the concept.

"We become our dreams," Simon explained. "You tell me what your dreams are and I'll tell you what sort of a person you are. Your dreams tell me not only what sort of a person you are today, but also what sort of person you aspire to be in the tomorrows of your life."

The interview lasted the whole hour and Simon took calls from all across the country.

Over and over, Simon gave powerful and potent examples of how the Dream Manager Program had application not only in the corporate world, but in marriage, parenting, friendship, politics, education, and every other arena of life and society.

"Helping people chase and fulfill their dreams is one of the primary functions of all relationships," he explained to one caller, "and this is true whether that relationship is between husband and wife, parent and child, or employer and employee."

Toward the end of the hour, Frank asked Simon, "What would you say to a business owner or corporate executive who is watching tonight?"

"Just this—the greatest problems we will face in corporate America in the next twenty years all surround the area of human resources, in particular, talent and labor. Executives will ignore these challenges at their peril. CEOs have to become as dedicated to scouting, nurturing, and acquiring talent as football coaches are. The future of any sporting franchise depends on the talent that takes the field. What makes you think your business is any different?"

Today

Today, five years after the birth of the initiative, more than 98 percent of Admiral employees participate in the Dream Manager Program. Home ownership among employees has tripled in five years, consumer debt among employees has been reduced by 40 percent . . . and 2,785 significant dreams have been accomplished.

Turnover has fallen from 400 percent to just 12 percent over the five-year period, and Admiral's internal placement program accounts for 70 percent of that turnover. Gross revenue has tripled, and the number of employees has risen from 407 to 743, including 11 Dream Managers. Profits have risen every quarter since the program was initiated.

Once a month, employees meet with the Dream Manager

in order to take time to dream up a richer, more abundant future for themselves and their families.

Today, the children twelve years and older of Admiral employees can meet with a Dream Manager once a month to discuss their future, their dreams . . .

Beginning next year, and as a result of the latest survey, the grandchildren fifteen years and older of employees will be able to meet with a Dream Manager once a month.

It seems we are never too young to start dreaming big dreams.

It's not hard to see why Admiral doesn't have a turnover problem anymore, is it?

At the last annual dinner for employees, Greg said in his speech, "Why are so many people so amazed by what we do here at Admiral? I ask myself this question all the time. Why is it so surprising to people to discover that if you treat people like people, they respond like people? Dreams are at the core of every person. It is there that our passion for life is ignited."

What's Your Dream?

As Simon walked into work, he paused in the lobby to read a plaque that had been there for more than a year now. Most days, he just walked straight past it because he knew what it said and he had things to do. But from time to time, he would force himself to stop and read it deliberately, as if for the first time, to refocus on the job at hand.

The plaque reads . . .

WHAT'S YOUR DREAM?

It's a question worth considering and a question that we should take the time to ask the people who are important to us.

In our corporate dealings, let us never forget that it is people who drive every business and organization. On both sides of every transaction, we find people. It is, therefore, people who decide whether corporations will be successful or unsuccessful . . . and people have dreams. In fact, the ability to dream is a big part of what makes us uniquely human.

The temptation is to convince yourself that your employees' dreams are not relevant to your business. That is only true if your employees are not relevant to your business—and if that were true, why would you employ them?

Most employees feel like they are being used. But if you can genuinely convince them that you have their best interests at heart, then you will reverse that belief, and in the process create a spirit of teamwork and loyalty rarely unleashed in the corporate world before now.

You can ignore people's dreams, but it will be at your peril. You are free to ignore your children's dreams, your spouse's dreams, your employees' dreams, your customers' dreams, and your nation's dreams. But in each of these areas of life, you will pay an enormous price if you do.

Dreams are invisible, but powerful. Think for a moment of electricity. You cannot see it, but it keeps everything going. Invisible, but powerful! If, for a moment, you doubt the power of electricity, consider what would happen if you stuck your finger into an electrical outlet. You would quickly be reminded of

its power. Should you doubt that electricity keeps everything going, may I suggest that you turn off the electricity at your office
tomorrow! I think you will find that little if anything gets done
and that most of your employees will go home for the day.

So it is with dreams. They are invisible, but powerful. You
cannot see them, but they keep everything going.

GETTING STARTED—
APPLICATIONS
AND TOOLS

WE LIVE IN the midst of a culture that constantly lusts for more of everything, including knowledge.

But the amassing of knowledge alone will not get us where we need to go. The real challenge lies in applying the truths we discover along the way to the various aspects of our lives and our organizations.

Wisdom is much more than the mere amassing of knowledge. Wisdom is truth lived.

This section has been designed as a practical guide to applying the concepts and principles of *The Dream Manager* to your team, organization, and life.

The First Truth

I have had many Dream Managers in my life. Parents and teachers, mentors and coaches, employers and colleagues, friends, and even the occasional stranger have all played the role to greater or lesser extents. Each of these people made considerable contributions to my journey, helped me along the way, and challenged me to explore the uncharted territory of my hopes and aspirations. Though, reflecting upon it all now, there is one who stands out. My first Dream Manager, in a more structured sense, was my brother Simon.

Simon is a financial planner, but in reality he is so much more than that. I have seven brothers and Simon is thirteen years my senior. When I was in my early teens, Simon would often take me out to a football game, to a movie, or for lunch.

He took an interest in who I was and who I wanted to become. It was during our little outings that I remember first formulating any real and concrete plans for the attainment of my dreams. He taught me that dreams often have a financial component. He taught me the compounding power of saving and investing. When I got my first job at twelve, delivering medications to the elderly for a local drugstore, both Simon and my father immediately encouraged me to embrace the discipline of saving. Simon also taught me that many dreams worth pursuing don't cost anything at all, and in this he taught me to value the simple and intangible things in life.

A decade later, as the Dream Manager concept began to take shape, I immediately recognized it as the evolution of something I had not only seen, but had experienced many years earlier.

If you look back on your life, I suspect you will also discover a variety of people—parents, grandparents, coaches, mentors, friends, employers, colleagues, supervisors, teachers, pastors, and others—who, to varying extents, have played the role of Dream Manager. More than likely, it occurred in a more organic and less formal way than the scheduled monthly meetings and the careful planning and documenting of specific dreams. Nonetheless, these people who took an interest in you and your aspirations no doubt had an enormous impact on your life.

Life seems to spontaneously supply these figures who challenge and encourage us in the direction of our dreams. "I can manage my own dreams!" many people exclaim. To a certain extent this is true, but we all need someone who can hold us accountable. Most of us can develop a plan for ourselves; it is the accountability that we struggle with. This accountability is absolutely critical to the process because we have an incredible ability to deceive ourselves with all manner of excuses and self-justifications.

We all need a Dream Manager. This is the first truth.

The Second Truth

In the various aspects and arenas of our lives, we also encounter other people who need to be challenged and encouraged in the direction of their dreams. In our personal and professional lives, we are constantly crossing paths with people who have dreams that are fallow or stagnant because nobody has encouraged them to clearly define those dreams and pursue them.

In the organic and less formal sense, we are all called to the role of Dream Manager. This is the second truth.

Whether you are the CEO of a multinational corporation, the manager of a small department, the newest member of a small corporate team, or a stay-at-home parent, you are called to be a Dream Manager in dozens of ways every day.

The question is: Where do we begin?

Begin Now—The First Step

Our dreams are the visions that shape our lives. Do you know what your dreams are? Have you stopped dreaming? Sometimes we do. At different points in our journey, both professionally and personally, it is easy to get so caught up in surviving that we stop dreaming. When we stop dreaming, we slowly begin to disengage from our work, from our relationships, and from life itself.

As a manager, it would be easy to read this book and immediately begin to focus on the dreams of the people you manage. To do this would be to miss a most critical step.

For more than a decade now, I have kept a Dream Book. I don't remember exactly how I came to this idea, but I do remember walking through a bookstore in Sydney in the early '90s and coming across a journal with thick, rough pages. I purchased it, though at the time I did not know why, as I had never kept a journal. As I flew to London a few days later, this simple journal was transformed into what I now call my Dream Book.

Since then, I have filled the pages with dreams. It is not a book of essays. On most pages, there is just one word or one phrase or one picture. The pages are filled with places I want to visit, personal and professional goals I want to accomplish, qualities I want to develop in my character, quotes that inspire me, the occasional fortune-cookie message, pictures torn from magazines of things I would like to own someday, hopes and dreams for the various organizations I am involved with, adventures I would like to take, the legacy I would like to create, and much more.

I take this small companion with me wherever I go. From time to time, on the plane, I will take it out and just flip through it slowly and ponder my dreams. Some nights, I read a few pages before I fall asleep. But on most days, I visit with my Dream Book while I am working out. For that hour, while I am on the treadmill or the elliptical, I just flip through the pages, reflecting upon my dreams, one at a time. Some have been accomplished long ago, and I like to remember how unattainable they seemed to me when I first wrote them down. Other dreams still seem distant and uncertain. Most of my dreams seemed that way when I first wrote them in the Dream Book. The dreams I have already accomplished give me the courage to chase the unaccomplished dreams. Passing through the pages, one dream at a time, I imagine how I will feel when I have achieved a particular dream, and I am constantly amazed at how this simple process begins the manifestation of my dreams.

Get yourself a Dream Book.
Start writing down your dreams.
Dream without limits.
Date your dreams as you add them to your Dream Book.
Date them again when you achieve them.

In time, you will look back on dreams you thought were impossible when you wrote them down and be amazed at the ease with which they were finally accomplished . . . and you will marvel at how much you have advanced in the journey.

One of the first dreams I wrote in my Dream Book, more than a decade ago, was to walk the Camino. The Camino is a five-hundred-mile walk. Beginning in Saint-Jean-Pied-de-Port, in southern France, one travels directly south across the Pyrenees and then due west across northern Spain to a place called Santiago. For more than a thousand years, people have been walking this path, and from the first time I heard of it, I was intrigued with the idea.

At the time, I went to write it in my Dream Book, but as I did, I remember thinking that I would probably never actually do it. My mind filled with questions and doubts. When will you be able to take a month off? Most people never take a month off. Who will take care of things while you are gone for a month? It's not practical. It could be dangerous. You will tell people, "I'm taking a month off!" and they will ask, "What are you going to do?" You will reply, "Take a walk!" and they will think you are crazy. For a moment, I hesitated. For a moment, I was not going to add this dream to the pages of my Dream Book, but I forced myself to write it down. That was more than eleven years ago now.

Day after day I would flip through the pages of my Dream Book and, over time, walking the Camino—along with so many other dreams—went from impossible, to maybe, to next year, to . . .

Last summer, I took a month off. I flew to southern France with a backpack, a map, a water bottle, a sleeping bag—and I started walking. I walked for twenty miles a day, twenty-five miles some days. Just walking—through the mountains, through the vineyards, through the cornfields, through the wheat fields, along the long, flat, dusty plains. Just walking for ten, twelve, sometimes fourteen hours a day. Walking. No cell phone, no e-mail, no iPod, no computer, no television, none of the things that fill our everyday lives.

Walking the old road to Santiago was a life-changing experience. At the end of the first day, I had walked thirty-one miles in silence and solitude. My mind was so fresh and so clear, brimming with ideas, and I remember thinking to myself that even if I stopped there and returned home at that very moment, I would never again be the same. By the time I walked into Santiago three weeks later, I wondered why I had waited so long to make this journey.

What are your dreams?

A five-hundred-mile walk may not be your idea of an exciting adventure. It doesn't matter. You have your own dreams to dream and your own adventures to pursue. Some time today, *drag yourself away* from all that occupies your daily attention and write down your dreams. Make a list of one hundred dreams. If you absolutely cannot do it today, at least take a moment to schedule it for tomorrow or the next day. And if you find yourself putting it off, ask yourself why.

The list does not have to be complete or perfect. You don't need a nice Dream Book with thick, rough pages. Just start writing. Don't place limitations on yourself. Dream and write from that stream of consciousness, as if anything were possible.

What has this got to do with managing people? What has this got to do with building a dynamic team? What has this got to do with running a business? I think you will be surprised.

As you write your Dream List, I offer you these twelve areas to stimulate a good cross section of dreams:

Physical
Emotional
Intellectual
Spiritual
Psychological
Material
Professional
Financial
Creative
Adventure
Legacy
Character

To further stimulate your dreaming, here are some examples of dreams that people have shared with me during the corporate retreats I conduct with my colleagues.

Physical
- look and feel healthy
- run a marathon
- quit smoking
- lose weight
- drink less

Emotional

- help my spouse and children discover and pursue their dreams
- buy my own home
- be in a great relationship
- take my spouse to Italy
- really try to listen more

Intellectual

- go back to school
- learn another language
- read more

Spiritual

- develop greater inner peace
- learn to enjoy uncertainty
- study the Scriptures

Psychological

- strengthen my willpower
- overcome my fear of flying
- face my addiction

Material

- get a new car
- buy my dream watch
- own a place by the beach

Professional
- get a promotion
- become #1 in the market
- build a dynamic team/department
- develop a new product
- reach $100 million in sales

Financial
- pay off credit-card debt
- start a college fund for my children
- earn $250,000 per year
- build a stock portfolio worth $1,000,000

Creative
- write a book
- learn to play guitar
- take a painting course
- study photography

Adventure
- visit the Great Wall of China
- visit Australia
- see U2 live in concert
- walk the Appalachian trail
- visit the Picasso museum in Paris
- go skydiving
- climb a 14,000-foot mountain

Legacy
- raise my children to have a healthy sense of who they are
- volunteer at my favorite charity
- donate to my favorite charity
- do my part to preserve the environment

Character
- develop patience
- do what I say I will do
- be respected for being completely trustworthy

It is important to note that some dreams may belong to more than one category. For example, paying off credit-card debt is financial, psychological, and emotional. Earning $250,000 a year could easily find itself in the professional and financial categories. Owning your own home has a financial element but also has a significant emotional component. Spending time with your children clearly has a place in the emotional realm but also has a legacy component.

These are just a few ideas to stimulate your imagination. You may choose to take some of these as your own and add others to them. Fine. Write your own list of one hundred dreams. Try to do it in one sitting. Nothing is too wild and wonderful. There are no limitations. Don't concern yourself with what you think is possible and what you think is not. Just write . . .

For the next week, take ten or fifteen minutes each day just to read through your Dream List. Other dreams may come to mind—add them! You may decide some dreams are not really you, or not that important to you. Delete them from the list if you wish, or leave them there so that you can look back in time and see what you thought was important to you.

After one week, go through the list and apply one of the following three categories to each of your dreams: short-term (within twelve months), mid-term (one to five years), or long-term (five years or more).

The next step is to get a Dream Book. You may not want to put all one hundred dreams straight into your Dream Book, but then again you may. There is no right or wrong way to do this. What is important is that you start to write down your dreams and ponder them from time to time so that you don't lose sight of them in the midst of your daily activity.

Over time, you may discover that you need more than one Dream Book. Today, I have one personal Dream Book, another professional Dream Book for my consulting company, and a third for my nonprofit foundation. One day, I hope to marry and have yet another Dream Book that my spouse and I share.

Get yourself a Dream Book!

Building a Dynamic Team

There are hundreds of team-building exercises, but many of them seem forced, and most people feel some level of discomfort participating. The key to successful team-building is creating a unity while celebrating the individuality of each member— common purpose colliding with unique contributions.

It is easy to focus on budgets and corporate goals, and too often our team gatherings revolve around these objectives. This quantitative-driven approach allows team members to learn more and more about what is driving the organization, but little about *what drives the people* who drive the organization.

Once a year, in November, I gather all of my staff for an informal afternoon together. I call it our annual Dream Session.

Each of my twelve staff members is asked to bring with them a list of one hundred dreams. Sitting around in the conference room, we spend the afternoon going from person to person, each team member sharing one dream each time around. Feedback, insight, and encouragement from the other team members begin an organic process of creating a strategy to achieve those dreams.

During this process, we also try to identify a time frame for each dream—within the next twelve months, one to five years, or five years or more. Each team member also reports on his or her progress over the past twelve months. All share their triumphs and trials, the dreams they achieved and those they failed to achieve.

New staff members often comment that this is the first time they have actually sat down and committed their dreams to paper. As other team members share their dreams, we often see the new staff reaching for their pens, making notes, and adding to their Dream Lists.

The passion of dreams is contagious. This is the passion that our teams need to be injected with. Get them passionate about their personal dreams and that passion will overflow into your organizational dreams.

It is amazing to discover people's dreams. Some of my employees' dreams are relatively simple, so much so that consciously acknowledging them and writing them down all but guarantees that a person will achieve them in the near future. These dreams tend to be manageable and achievable without much planning or preparation; it is simply a matter of making them a priority. Others are complex and much more involved. These dreams tend to require significant planning and constant vigilance if they are to be attained.

Year after year, as I sit there listening, I am amazed at some of my employees' dreams. In some cases, I have been working with these people for years, yet still they manage to surprise me.

What strikes me most, however, is not what happens during the Dream Session, but what happens casually and informally in the weeks and months that follow. I overhear them talking to each other about their dreams, asking each other what progress they are making with a particular dream, and encouraging each other to keep at it. In small ways and large, they begin to help each other to live their dreams, and this spirit of cooperation naturally overflows into their work together as a team.

I also find myself thinking about their dreams. We will be in a staff meeting or working together on a project, and I will catch myself wondering, *How can I help him live that dream?* or *Which of her dreams can I help her accomplish this year?*

The best part of all this is that I don't think my response—a desire to help my staff members achieve their dreams—is extraordinary. I think it is human. *When we know the dreams of*

the people around us, we want to help them live those dreams.
There is something incredibly fulfilling about helping someone else achieve a dream.

This process, which is disarmingly simple and seemingly
far-removed from anything to do with business, changes me as
a manager, changes my people as employees, and transforms us
collectively as a team. It creates a unique intimacy that gives
birth to an extraordinarily dynamic type of teamwork.

In January, I hold staff reviews and I encourage each of my
employees to bring their list of one hundred dreams to their
review. As part of their review, I like to talk to them about
their dreams, and during that meeting I try to pinpoint one
dream that I can help them achieve in the coming year. Sometimes it is a simple thing, something that can be easily attained.
At other times, the dream requires considerable planning.

Bethany Hawkins is one of my event coordinators. She is
responsible for managing my visits to more than one hundred
cities in the United States each year, and she does an amazing
job. She is dedicated, loyal, passionate about what we do, and
relentlessly committed to continuous improvement and excellence. The days on the road are long and filled with challenges
and pressures. So when my team and I are not on the road, we
each need to find ways to be rejuvenated.

Last year, during our Dream Session, Bethany mentioned
that she would like to volunteer in a school, teaching children
to read. Within a month, we had made arrangements for her to
have a few hours off each Thursday morning to volunteer in a
school not too far from our offices. She can check that dream

off her list ... and move on to the other ninety-nine. Each week, she leaves the office for two hours to live a dream, but you can be sure our work is better off because she does.

I want a team full of people dedicated to pursuing their personal dreams. If they cannot be passionate about their own lives, how can I reasonably expect them to be passionate about our work?

Sara McClure is another example. She is twenty-five years old, remarkably capable, and has a wonderful "can-do" attitude. Sara manages all the responsibilities of our front office. The dream that jumped out at me on her list at our last Dream Session was: to spend a month in Europe. Having done just that myself the summer before, I was particularly committed to helping her to live this dream.

I got the rest of my staff together and floated the idea that perhaps we should help Sara accomplish this dream sooner rather than later, and asked them to give it some thought and come back to me. A week later, they came back to me with a plan. Those closest to Sara had discovered that she had been saving for the trip and was in good stead financially. Bridget, who organizes much of our travel, suggested that with our travel contacts we could get her a cheap airfare. Beth explained that she was eligible for some vacation and suggested we could offer her leave without pay for the remainder of the time. And Walter suggested that she could go in July, which is the quietest month of the year anyway.

"That's great!" I said. "Who will do her work while she is gone?" They took out a document that outlined Sara's roles and responsibilities, which they had divided among themselves and had agreed to cover for the month she was gone.

In the summer, less than twelve months after her first Dream Session, and just over a year after joining our team, Sara spent a month in Europe and had an extraordinary experience. How do you think she feels about the people she works with? How do you think she feels about the organization she works for?

I could tell you dozens of stories of dreams that have been identified, pursued, and achieved through this process—some team members wanted a new watch or a new car, others wanted to buy their first home, and others still, hoped to improve a relationship with a spouse or a child. Identifying their dreams and being supported in their dreams by their coworkers has animated the people I work with, both personally and professionally, and in the process has transformed them into a team that thrives on dynamic collaboration.

The reasons are simple.

First, when we know the dreams of the people around us, we want to help them live those dreams. In helping them live their dreams, we become personally invested in them—one of the fundamentals of teamwork.

Second, nothing animates people like chasing down a dream. The passion and energy that are the telltale signs of this animation cannot be confined to one area of our lives. Both the positive and the negative of our personal and professional lives flow freely between our life at home and our life at work. When people are chasing their dreams personally, the positive energy that is generated spills over into their professional lives.

And finally, helping someone else accomplish a dream gives us a satisfaction that rivals the fulfillment we experience when we achieve our own dreams. People are enormously grateful to the people who help them live their dreams, and that gratitude between team members makes them willing to go the extra mile for one another.

An organization changes when the habits of the people who make up that organization change. *Get your people in the habit of pursuing and achieving dreams in their personal lives and they will be much more effective at chasing down the goals and dreams you place before them in the workplace.* Achieving dreams is a habit.

I have worked with Fortune 500 companies and small, family-owned businesses, football teams and nonprofit organizations, trade associations and colleges, and I have never worked with a team that didn't benefit massively from the Dream Session exercise.

Universally Applicable

When I first began to describe the Dream Manager Program to people, some told me that it would only work with unskilled labor, others said that it would only work with a company's best people, and some people were certain that the corporate world would never subscribe to such an employee enrichment program. I am delighted to say that all of these naysayers were wrong.

Wherever there are people, the concept and principles of the Dream Manager will work powerfully, because people have dreams, and nothing animates people and teams like the pursuit of a dream.

Beyond that, living your dreams is often about facing your fears and rising to the challenge. This becomes abundantly apparent once a team has been in the Dream Manager Program for any period of time.

In the beginning, their dreams tend to fall into two categories:

1. Easily attainable and well within reach
2. Completely unrealistic in any predictable period of time

Both of these are seen as being equally safe because they don't stretch us in any way that makes us accountable to them.

Over time, however, as people achieve some of their dreams, their confidence builds and they begin to acknowledge those interim dreams that build the bridge between the dreams we have already achieved and the dreams that seem completely unattainable at first. With the pursuit and attainment of every dream, however small or seemingly insignificant, people develop skills for identifying, chasing, and accomplishing goals and dreams. In most cases, these skills would not be developed in a corporate setting even over a whole lifetime. Perhaps more importantly, as people accomplish dreams, they develop a hunger for the accomplishment of more dreams.

Help your employees develop goal-setting and strategic-planning skills by chasing their personal dreams, and they will gladly bring these skills to their work because they cannot help but bring them. The hunger to achieve goals and dreams becomes almost insatiable, the desire for continuous improvement becomes a guiding force in their daily lives, and all of this will inevitably overflow into their work, and in the process, will elevate your team and your business.

The concept of management by dreams provides unlimited application possibilities for every organization, and also holds extraordinary possibilities for our personal lives. Here are just a few of the ideas and applications that demonstrate the diversity of the Dream Manager concept.

FINANCIAL PLANNERS

No professional group is better positioned to apply these principles to their work than financial planners. Your clients' dreams provide rare insights into their philosophy about life and money, and, in turn, empower you to manage their money most effectively for the fulfillment of their dreams. Knowledge of their dreams also enables you to challenge clients to save and invest with more discipline.

The reality is, most dreams have a financial component. Whether someone dreams of buying a new car, retiring early, or spending more time pursuing a passion, a financial plan is necessary if the dream is to be accomplished. The other point to consider here is that most people think that the only thing that lies between where they are today and the fulfillment of their dreams is money. So who better to help you put together a plan for the fulfillment of your dreams (at least those that have a financial component) than your financial advisor?

If you are a financial planner, you may want to think about

having your clients put together a Dream List. It will help you get to know your clients, and it will demonstrate that you are interested in helping them build a future. By engaging them in a dialogue about their dreams, you will immediately achieve a customer intimacy that would take years to develop under normal circumstances.

Once a client has put together a Dream List, you can pick some milestone dreams and develop a plan around them. Retirement lifestyle is the obvious one, but there may also be several smaller, nearer-term dreams that need to be planned for if they are going to be accomplished and enjoyed. Regardless of the dreams, it will be significantly easier to get your clients to commit to the discipline of money management if they have a clear vision of the dreams they are working toward.

There is only one good reason to amass money and that is for the fulfillment of a dream. Peter Thornhill, the Australian investment strategist, in his book *Motivated Money*, reminds his readers that *"Making money without having a dream to fulfill is pointless and obscene."* Most Americans today spend more money each year than they earn, descending further and further into debt. Collectively, Americans save less than one penny for every dollar they earn. Why do people save so little? The answer, I believe, is because they don't know what their dreams are—and without a clear vision of their dreams, they simply fail to see the point of saving.

The principles and tools of the Dream Manager concept hold the power to completely revolutionize the financial planning industry; let it begin with your business.

EDUCATION

Teachers, coaches, guidance counselors, mentors, and, of course, parents, are all Dream Managers, to varying extents. Their role in the lives of young people is to help them discover their unique abilities, identify their hopes and dreams, and encourage them to pursue these dreams in a way that makes a contribution to society and humanity.

We seem to be in a great hurry to rush young people into one career or another, without having taken the time to help them determine what they are best suited to. We seem too eager to clutter their minds with all types of facts and figures, instead of instilling in them a real sense of self. The result is the very discontentment that leads to disengagement in the workplace and in life.

Imagine how your life may have been different if someone had taken the time, when you were young, to help you understand the twelve areas: physical, emotional, intellectual, spiritual, psychological, material, professional, financial, creative, adventure, legacy, and character. Imagine if someone had walked you through specific exercises in each of these areas, helping you to discover your strengths and weaknesses; your interests and passions; and the people, places, and things that energize you. Imagine.

How might your life have been different if you had had a Dream Manager in high school or college?

By helping young people discover these things about themselves, we will produce a new breed of worker for the future— a workforce that is super-engaged, highly effective, immensely responsible, self-aware, intuitive, and motivated. Wouldn't you like a handful of employees like this at your company?

Every young person should have a Dream Manager.

FAST FOOD

Flipping burgers has been the center of cultural jokes for decades now, and few industries have a more *actively disengaged* workforce than the fast-food industry. Turnover in this industry can make or break a franchise.

Can the Dream Manager work with the employees of fast-food chains? Is it even possible to engage these employees?

When my brother Bernard graduated from high school, his grades were not that great. About a week before his last exam, he asked me what I thought he should do. I suggested that he might want to think about working for McDonald's. I knew a couple of guys who had gone through their management program and I had been impressed with the training they had received. I also knew that while Bernard wasn't an academic genius, he was intuitive, had a remarkable gift with people, and could memorize certain things in a way that was uncanny. All this led me to believe that he would thrive in an environment that revolved around people but was run with systems.

Bernard went through his management program faster than anyone in history, became the youngest store manager in Australia's corporate stores, took a store that was losing more than half a million dollars annually and turned a profit of $200,000 in less than a year, became the youngest manager of the largest store in Sydney, and built a personal stock portfolio valued at more than $100,000 before the age of twenty-four.

Today, he works for McDonald's as a consultant to a cluster of their downtown city stores in Sydney.

He is twenty-seven years old, and you have never seen anybody more passionate about McDonald's. He can tell you everything there is to know about the history of the organization and he understands the business model completely. Bernard demands more of himself and more of his staff than most, and he rarely disappoints or is disappointed.

What is the difference between Bernard and the thousands of men and women managing fast-food stores around the world, beating their heads against a wall trying to engage their minimum-wage employees? Bernard takes a keen interest in his people. He doesn't have time to sit around and talk all day, but he will take a few moments here and there to get to know the people on his team, particularly their dreams. He isn't foolish enough to believe that his employees will be there forever, so he talks to them about their lives, their futures. From time to time, he photocopies a page or two from a book that he thinks will be helpful to them. He encourages people, he challenges people, and they respond because his sincerity is palpable and many of them have never had someone take such an interest in them.

Every time "corporate" sent him to a new store, it was a store that needed turning around. They sent him because they knew he would get the job done. Bernard would arrive at the store with goals and a plan. He would announce his goals to everybody on the team, from the assistant store managers to the crew members mopping the floors. He constantly reminded his team of these goals and he united them in a common purpose.

"Whatever you're doing, you'll feel better about yourself and life if you do it well," I overheard him saying to some of his team members one day. It was one of his mantras.

I always smile to myself when I hear people making fun of people who work at McDonald's because I've seen the world and met an awful lot of people, but I don't know many who have tasted the passion Bernard has for his work or the satisfaction he gets from working hard and being successful.

His approach creates a collaborative team, a dynamic environment, and extraordinary results, and minimizes turnover.

The only thing costing the fast-food industry more than the people who leave (turnover) is some of the employees who stay (*the actively disengaged*). Show your employees how flipping burgers can help them achieve a dream and you will engage them in a way many have long believed to be impossible in this industry.

· · ·

Financial planning, education, fast food—these are just a handful of the industries and arenas that could benefit massively from the Dream Manager concept. I would love to write whole books about how these ideas could translate into health care, banking, and a dozen other industries. There is no end to the possibilities that exist for the Dream Manager. From industry to industry, from one company to the next, the practical applications are immense.

No Company Program

You may be reading this book thinking, *I would love a Dream Manager, but my company will never go for this!* You may be saying to yourself, "I wish my company had a Dream Manager Program, but I'm not a manager. I'm just an employee!"

If your company doesn't have a Dream Manager Program, or won't start one, start it yourself! Gather a small group of employees—coworkers—not more than perhaps eight. Meet with this small group once a week, before work or during your lunch break. Talk about your dreams. Get a Dream Book. Make a Dream List. Begin to develop plans and timelines. Follow the Dream Manager Program if you wish. Encourage each other. Keep each other accountable. When you need professional advice (financial, legal, fitness, diet, etc.), seek it.

Before long, others will want to join. Split your group in two groups of four, and allow four new members to join each group. New people with different dreams give us new perspectives on our own dreams and renew our enthusiasm to chase our dreams.

You will be amazed how a commitment to this simple process will transform your life and the lives of your colleagues. Begin now. You don't need to be a manager. All you need is two or more people who have dreams!

A New Breed of Loyalty

There are many who say that loyalty in the corporate world is dead forever. I could not disagree with them more. The kind of corporate loyalty that was based on hanging around for a certain number of years in order to get a pension and benefits for the rest of your life may be dead, but I think that both employees and employers are better off that it is. It wasn't good for people or companies then, and it isn't good for people or companies now. I do, however, believe that the corporate world desperately needs to foster and encourage a new and more evolved form of corporate loyalty.

This new breed of loyalty will be built on the principle of *adding value*. An employee *is responsible* for adding value to the life of a company, and a company *is responsible* for adding value to the life of an employee. This is the great unspoken contract that exists between all employees and employers.

There is an inescapable financial component to the principle of adding value in business. A potential employee should be able to walk into an interview and confidently say, "Hire me and I will generate three . . . five . . . seven times more revenue than it costs to employ me." This is one of the ways employees are responsible for adding value. Part of adding value in a corporate environment means generating revenue or supporting someone else so they can generate revenue.

As I walked out of a keynote presentation several months ago, the president of the company took me aside and said, "I just want to thank you for adding value. I know this is going to help my people take it to the next level." His words gave me pause. People often say, "Great talk," but as I reflected on what he had said to me, it crystallized a realization that when I speak at corporate events, I'm not there *just* to motivate, entertain, and inspire. I aim to do those things, but I am there to add value—to help that company and its employees thrive. That is why companies invite me to speak, and if I cannot do that, I cannot reasonably expect them to invite me back.

A new breed of corporate loyalty is both possible and necessary. We simply need to change our expectations. No company can keep an employee that doesn't add value and help that company become the-best-version-of-itself. Simple economics demands that such an employee cannot remain. At the same time, a company cannot reasonably expect an employee to be loyal, if that company's demands and expectations consistently lead an employee to become a lesser-version-of-himself or herself.

The new breed of loyalty will be based upon an understanding between employees and companies of one another's purpose—to become the-best-version-of-themselves. Some may scoff and beg this conversation to return to reality—but consider the companies that find themselves on Fortune's elite list of the best companies to work for. Of course they strive for and achieve better than average profits, but if you glance down the list of criteria, you'll discover a list of company initiatives that, directly or indirectly, help employees become better-versions-of-themselves. These companies believe that if they help their employees become better-versions-of-themselves, the company will necessarily become a-better-version-of-itself.

Walk through the hallways of these companies and you will see a highly evolved form of corporate loyalty emerging. These companies understand that if they help their employees achieve their purpose as individuals, the employees will in turn be more passionate about helping the corporation achieve its purpose and goals. Both sides recognize that the company has to make a profit in order to continue, and both sides are willing to commit to the pursuit of that profit.

This new breed of corporate loyalty is the clay from which a highly evolved and cohesive type of team can be built and managed. The "us versus them" mentality that has been fostered for hundreds of years in the workplace desperately needs to be replaced by a spirit of dynamic collaboration. This level of collaboration can only be achieved when both managers and employees are convinced that each has the others' best interests in mind.

Sooner or later, both a company and its employees will gravitate toward their respective purposes. If they cannot do this in collaboration, employees will begin to disengage or self-destruct and the organization will pay a huge price.

When a company's culture opposes its employees' purpose (that is, hinders employees from becoming the-best-version-of-themselves), the employees will consciously or subconsciously oppose the company's goals and objectives. This in turn will prevent the company from achieving its purpose (that is, becoming the-best-version-of-itself). The individual purposes of employees and companies are inseparably linked.

A manager's role is to organize employee effort for the attainment of an organization's goals and purpose. In the past, managers have relied heavily on the stick and the carrot. Now it is time to discover the awesome effectiveness of management by dreams.

The Twenty-First-Century Manager

Managing people has perhaps never been a more daunting task. This is true whether you are a CEO, the leader of a small department, or a parent. Even managing ourselves has become increasingly complex and difficult in the midst of a modern schema filled with endless possibilities and opportunities. From where will clarity emerge? The answer is from a deep and resounding understanding of our purpose, both as people and as organizations.

The modern manager is responsible for helping an organization become the-best-version-of-itself. The major objective of this role has never changed. Only now, the modern manager understands that achieving this objective is largely dependent on a team of employees dedicated to becoming better-versions-of-themselves.

The most effective leaders and managers will be those who find ways to advance a company, while at the same time helping employees to advance personally and professionally.

If a manager attempts to advance the company's purpose to the detriment of the employees' purpose, it will hurt both employee and company. On the other hand, advance the employees' purpose at the detriment of the company, and it will hurt both company and employee. The two must find a way to coexist in support of one another. The two must find ways to add value in equal measure.

For decades, we have invested billions of corporate dollars in programs that pretend to focus on employee enrichment, but in truth were designed to get exactly what the corporation wanted. Why are we surprised that these programs are met with cynicism and that the results are mediocre? Corporate leaders often display the very same cynicism when programs are proposed that actually focus on employee enrichment, doubting that the payoff will be there for the company.

In all of this, we have overlooked the startling reality that if you play a role in teaching your employees how to manage *their* money, they will manage *your* money more effectively and be less distracted by personal financial concerns. If you play a role in helping your employees to adopt a healthy lifestyle, your health insurance costs will be reduced and your employees will be more effective because they are healthier. The examples are endless.

Rule #1—You cannot reasonably expect people to do for your company what they won't do for themselves.

Hire an accountant who doesn't manage his personal finances well, and you are asking for trouble. Hire an employee-relations executive who doesn't generally get along with people in her personal life, and you are asking for trouble.

I work all the time with CEOs who are baffled that they can't get their senior managers to really throw themselves into the strategic-planning process. "They constantly want breaks to check e-mail and voice mail," one CEO said to me recently.

And yet, when you examine the lives of these senior managers, you discover they spend more time planning their annual vacation than they spend planning their lives.

One of the most powerful exercises we facilitate in our two-day executive retreats is to take each member of an executive team through a process that helps them create a Personal Strategic Plan. We begin by examining the twelve areas—physical, emotional, intellectual, spiritual, psychological, material, professional, financial, creative, adventure, legacy, and character. We then take traditional strategic-planning methods and exercises and apply them to the different areas of a team member's life, helping him/her to create a three-year Personal Strategic Plan with specific and measurable Critical Success Factors.

Many of these people have been putting together strategic plans for their organizations or departments for decades, but have never created a Personal Strategic Plan. Once we have taken them through the process—made it personal—their involvement in corporate strategic planning takes on a whole new meaning, and is usually accompanied by a whole new level of enthusiasm.

Teach them the importance of strategic planning in their own lives and they will understand its importance in the life of your company. The same is true for dreams and goals. If you want to engage employees in corporate dreams and goals, you must first engage them in their own personal dreams and goals.

So, you're a manager. You picked up the book, and you like the idea, but where do you start? Here are four first steps.

Step One

Write your own Dream List. Examine each of the twelve areas and come up with a list of one hundred dreams.

Step Two

Spend half an hour each morning walking around, visiting with your team members. Begin to take a sincere interest in their work and their lives.

Step Three

Pull your team together for a Dream Session. Send out a memo or call a meeting to explain what it is, how it will work, and what it is designed to achieve. If you are concerned about how it will be received, have some or all of your team members read this book before the Dream Session.

Step Four

Use employee reviews as an opportunity to take an interest in the dreams of the people who report to you. Try to pinpoint one dream you can help and encourage each team member to accomplish in the next twelve months. At the same time, use this as an opportunity to educate individual team members about the dreams you have for your company, department, team, or project.

Launching the Dream Manager Program formally at your company is something you should consider, but whether or not you pursue the program formally you should begin its *informal* implementation *today*. It will cost you nothing, and you will begin to see results almost immediately.

Dreams provide fascinating insights into what drives people. This is indispensable knowledge for a manager of any kind.

Take an active interest in the dreams of the people on your team and in your life, encourage them to move boldly in the direction of their dreams, and have the courage to share your own personal and professional dreams with them. Over time, the people who surround you will begin to do the same among themselves, and you will witness a new spirit of collaboration—and the unrivaled power of a culture of dreams.

It is a different approach, I must admit, and I feel certain that you will agree with me. I am equally certain that *different is exactly what is needed* in the corporate arena if we are going to engage employees and build dynamic teams. So, I beg you—*don't be ordinary!* Not as a manager, not as a friend, not as a lover, not as a parent, not as an employee, and not as a citizen. Don't be ordinary . . .

Acknowledgments

LIFE IS ABOUT dreams. As human beings we have the unique capacity to look into the future, envision something, and then act on the present to bring our vision to reality. My life has been filled with so many dreams come true, and for that there are many people I am grateful to. To all my Dream Managers—past, present, and future—thanks for giving me one of life's most precious gifts, your time. You are my coaches, friends, teachers, pastors, brothers, role models, heroes, parents . . . and the occasional stranger providentially crossing my path. You have helped me live my dreams and comforted me when my dreams have been crushed and broken. Thank you.

To my readers . . . what a privilege it is to write for you. I am honored and humbled that in a world where altogether too many books are published, you choose to buy and read my writings. You will never know the gratitude in my heart.

To the ambassadors . . . those rare people who not only read my books but set about on a mission to share them with everyone who crosses their paths. Thank you for inviting me into your circle of influence.

In particular, I would like to thank . . . My father for igniting in me a passion for business. My brother Simon for teaching me about goal setting and planning. Tony Miller, you are a genius. Pat Lencioni, your support and encouragement are like a breath of fresh air. Bethany Hawkins for reading, and reading, and rereading the manuscript. Dan Brunnert and my colleagues at Beresford Consulting. And finally . . . the man who has single-handedly restored my faith in publishing, Will Schwalbe, it has been an absolute pleasure to work with you.

Something wonderful is about to happen!

About the Author

MATTHEW KELLY is an internationally acclaimed speaker and author, and the president of Floyd Consulting, a consulting firm founded on the belief that your organization can only become the-best-version-of-itself to the extent that the people who drive your organization are striving to become better-versions-of-themselves.

Kelly's books have sold more than one million copies and have appeared on the *New York Times*, *Wall Street Journal*, *USA Today*, *Publishers Weekly*, and numerous other best-seller lists. His other titles include *The Rhythm of Life: Living Every Day with Passion and Purpose* and *The Seven Levels of Intimacy*.

More than three million people in fifty countries have attended Kelly's presentations and seminars. Over the past decade, he has given over 2,500 keynote presentations at conferences and conventions for a wide variety of organizations, including

Fortune 500 companies, national trade associations, professional organizations, universities, churches, and nonprofit organizations. Against the backdrop of his travel to fifty countries, millions more individuals have been touched by his writings and appearances on radio and television programs.

With his keen sense of humor and passion for helping companies understand that developing their employees is the first step to achieving corporate goals, Kelly seems to effortlessly elevate and energize people to pursue the highest values of the human spirit.

Matthew Kelly's message is both timely and timeless. His example is authentic and inspiring. His passion for life is refreshing and challenging. It is certain he will continue to be, with increasing influence, one of the most sought-after and enduring voices of our time.

The Dream Manager Program

THE DREAM MANAGER PROGRAM is the ultimate life coaching program designed to help individuals and companies identify and pursue their dreams. Floyd Consulting works with organizations of all sizes to implement the program.

For Companies

If you would like to discuss the possibility of introducing the Dream Manager Program to your organization, please contact us at Floyd Consulting.

For Individuals

We also provide a program for individuals whose companies do not currently offer the Dream Manager Program for their employees. If you are interested in participating in the program as an individual, please visit *www.thedreammanager.com* or call 312-698-5025.

Employment Opportunities

We are always looking for Dream Managers to join our team. If you believe your skills, personality, and experience lend themselves to this role, we would love to hear from you.

What's Your Dream?

At Floyd Consulting, we are dedicated to helping people live their dreams. Tell us your dream! Throughout the year, the Floyd team selects a handful of dreams from those submitted and helps to make them happen. Submit your dream today at *www.thedreammanager.com*.

Floyd Consulting, Inc.

FLOYD CONSULTING is home to the Dream Manager Program and was founded on the idea that the destinies of organizations and the people who drive them are intertwined. An organization will only become the-best-version-of-itself to the extent that the people who drive that organization are becoming better-versions-of-themselves.

Teamwork and talent remain the ultimate competitive advantages. Floyd Consulting helps organizations do two things:

- attract, develop, nurture, and retain the *right* people, and
- build, manage, and motivate dynamic teams

Whether you are the head coach of an NFL football team, a small business owner, the CEO of a Fortune 500 company, or the director of a nonprofit organization, we will help you to attract the talent, build the team, and create the strategy that you need to take your organization to the next level.

Floyd Consulting serves CEOs, executive teams, managers, individual departments, and entire companies. Whether your need is a keynote presentation, an off-site retreat, strategic planning, or the implementation of the Dream Manager Program, let Floyd Consulting customize a program to fit your needs.

For more information contact:

Floyd Consulting, Inc.
1235A North Clybourn, #109
Chicago, IL 60610
312-698-5025
www.thedreammanager.com